FRAMEWORKS OF GEOGRAPHY
DECODABLE GRAPHIC NOVEL

INTRODUCTION TO MAPS

Written by Izzi Howell

Illustrated by Steve Evans

CHERRY LAKE PRESS

a Scott Fetzer company
Chicago

Published in the United States of America by Cherry Lake Publishing Group
Ann Arbor, Michigan
www.cherrylakepublishing.com

Produced in partnership with World Book, Inc.
World Book, Inc.
180 North LaSalle Street
Suite 900
Chicago, Illinois 60601
USA

Illustrator: Steve Evans
Decodable Text Adaptation: Cherry Lake Press

Additional spot art by Shutterstock

Text Copyright © 2025 by Cherry Lake Publishing Group
Illustrations Copyright © 2023 by World Book, Inc.
All rights reserved. No part of this book may be reproduced or utilized
in any form or by any means without written permission from the publisher.

Cherry Lake Press is an imprint of Cherry Lake Publishing Group.

Library of Congress Cataloging-in-Publication Data has been filed and is
available at catalog.loc.gov.

Cherry Lake Publishing Group would like to acknowledge the work of the
Partnership for 21st Century Learning, a Network of Battelle for Kids.
Please visit Battelle for Kids online for more information.

Printed in the United States of America

TABLE OF CONTENTS

What Is a Map? 4
Types of Maps 6
Map Scales 10
Map Symbols and Legends 14
Map Compass 18
Topographic Maps 20
Grid Reference System 22
Latitude and Longitude 24
Maps and Globes 28
How Maps Are Made 32
Maps Today 36
Can You Believe It?! 38
Words to Know 40

There is a glossary on page 40. Terms defined in the glossary
are in type **that looks like this** on their first appearance.
Pronunciations can be found alongside their first appearance.

WHAT IS A MAP?

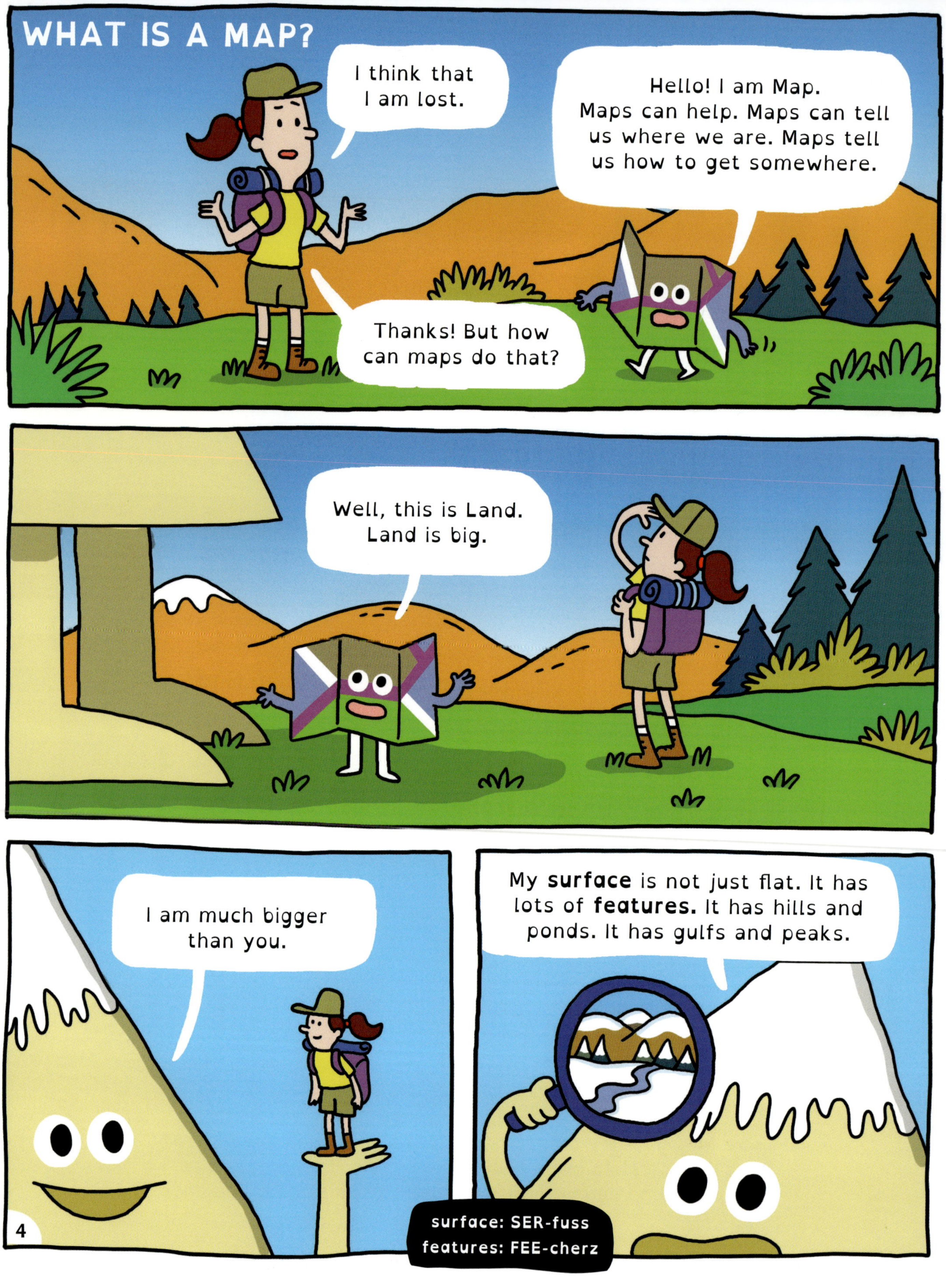
I think that I am lost.
Hello! I am Map. Maps can help. Maps can tell us where we are. Maps tell us how to get somewhere.
Thanks! But how can maps do that?
Well, this is Land. Land is big.
I am much bigger than you.
My **surface** is not just flat. It has lots of **features.** It has hills and ponds. It has gulfs and peaks.

surface: SER-fuss
features: FEE-cherz

I can get lost on land! It is THAT big!
Maps can tell us which features land has. A map is a drawing. Maps show land features in a simple way. Maps help us find things.
Aha! I can tell that I am in this spot!
A pond is on this map. This map tells us its size and shape.
This map tells how far it is to this shop.
This bench is not on that map.
Maps will not tell us everything that is on land. Maps with too much on them can get confusing. That will not help.
Maps tell us **important** things. That is how maps can help.

important: im-POR-tunt

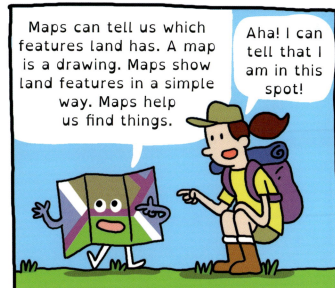

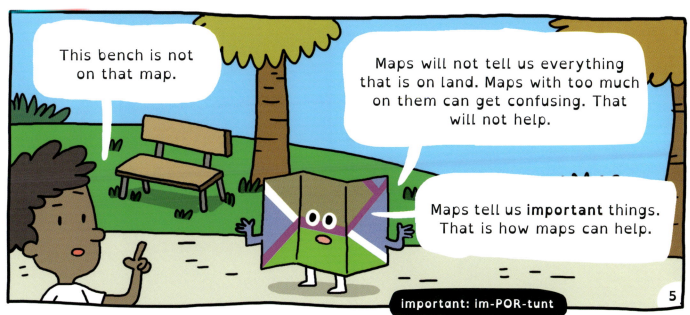

TYPES OF MAPS

Cartographers make maps. Different maps tell us different things.
cartographers: car-TAH-gruff-erz
Road maps tell us which path will get us somewhere. Lines on this map show roads.
Maps can show hills and paths in forests.
Transit maps tell us bus and train routes. This map helps us get around town.

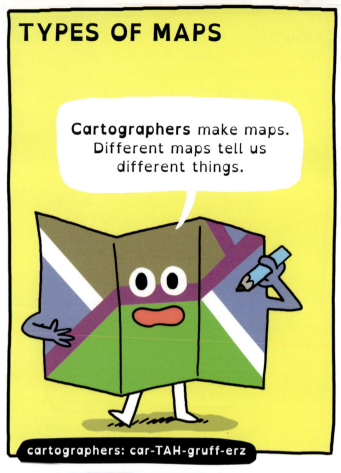

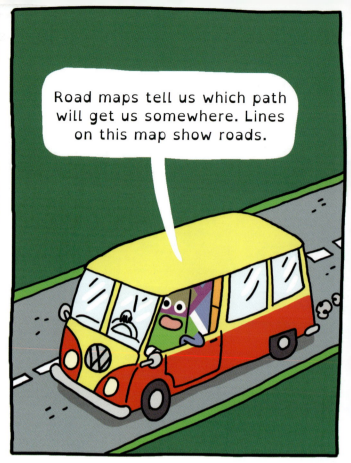

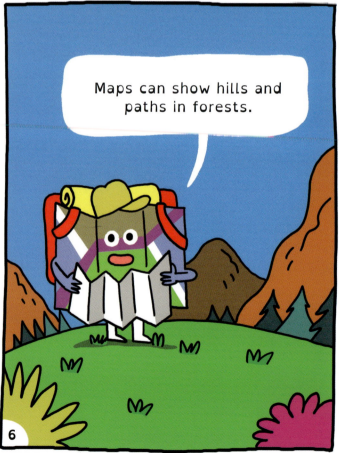

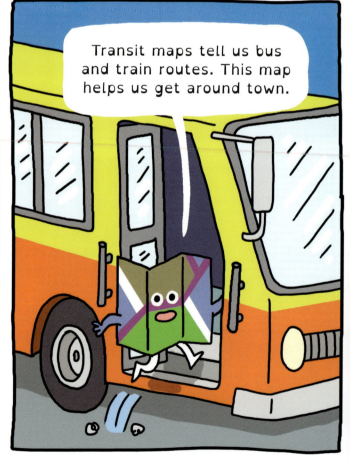

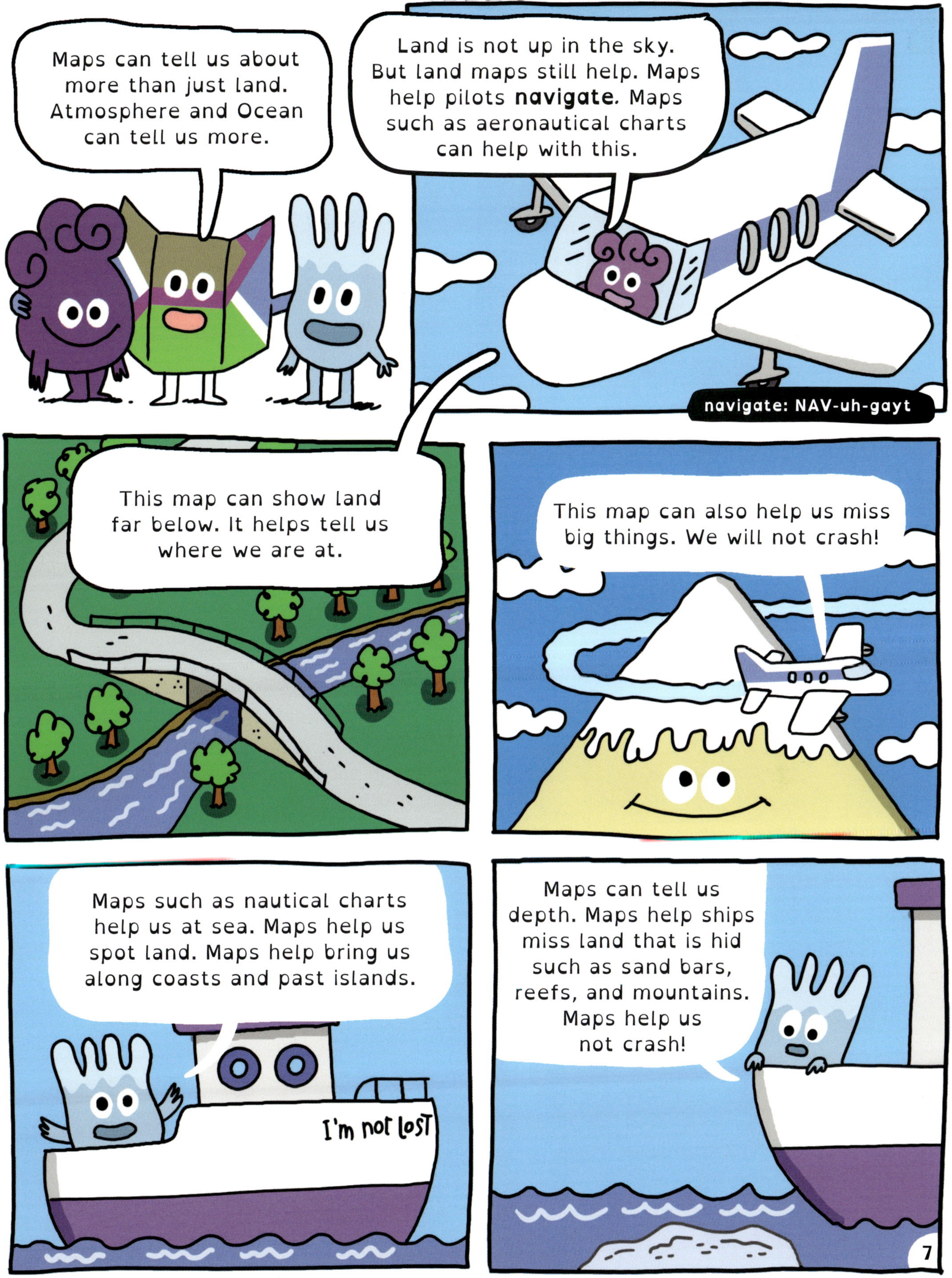
Maps can tell us about more than just land. Atmosphere and Ocean can tell us more.
Land is not up in the sky. But land maps still help. Maps help pilots **navigate**. Maps such as aeronautical charts can help with this.
navigate: NAV-uh-gayt
This map can show land far below. It helps tell us where we are at.
This map can also help us miss big things. We will not crash!
Maps such as nautical charts help us at sea. Maps help us spot land. Maps help bring us along coasts and past islands.
I'm not lost
Maps can tell us depth. Maps help ships miss land that is hid such as sand bars, reefs, and mountains. Maps help us not crash!

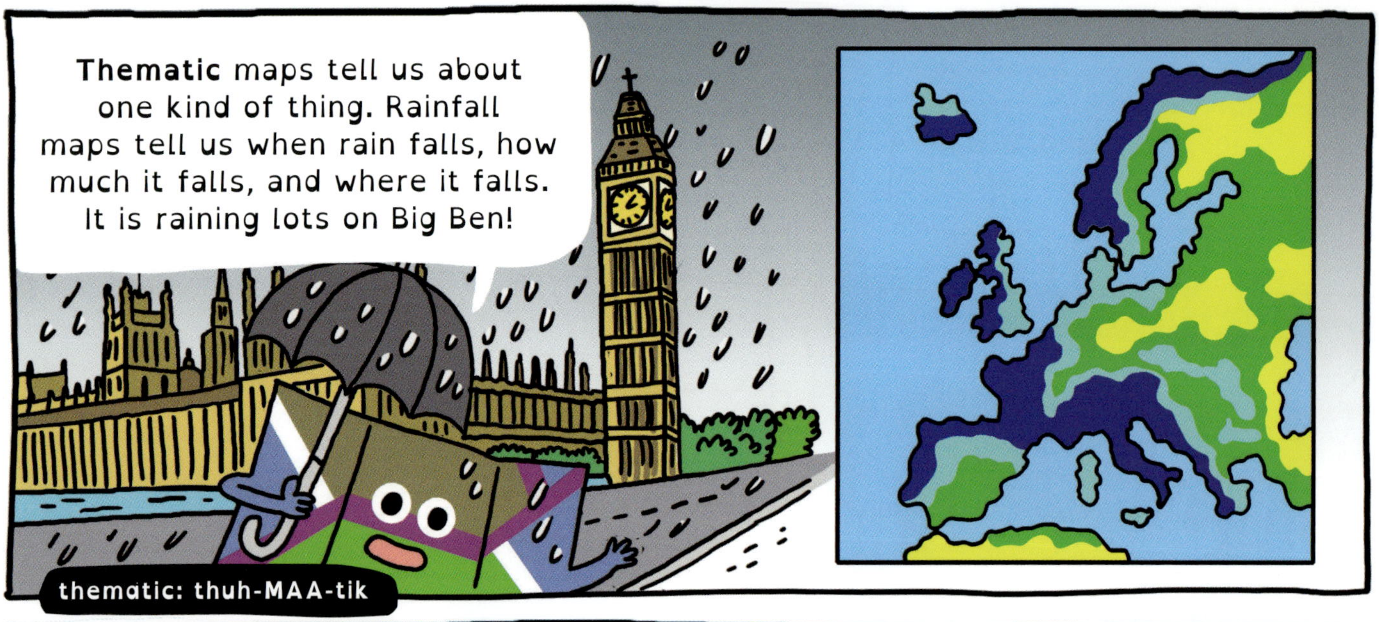
Thematic maps tell us about one kind of thing. Rainfall maps tell us when rain falls, how much it falls, and where it falls. It is raining lots on Big Ben!
thematic: thuh-MAA-tik

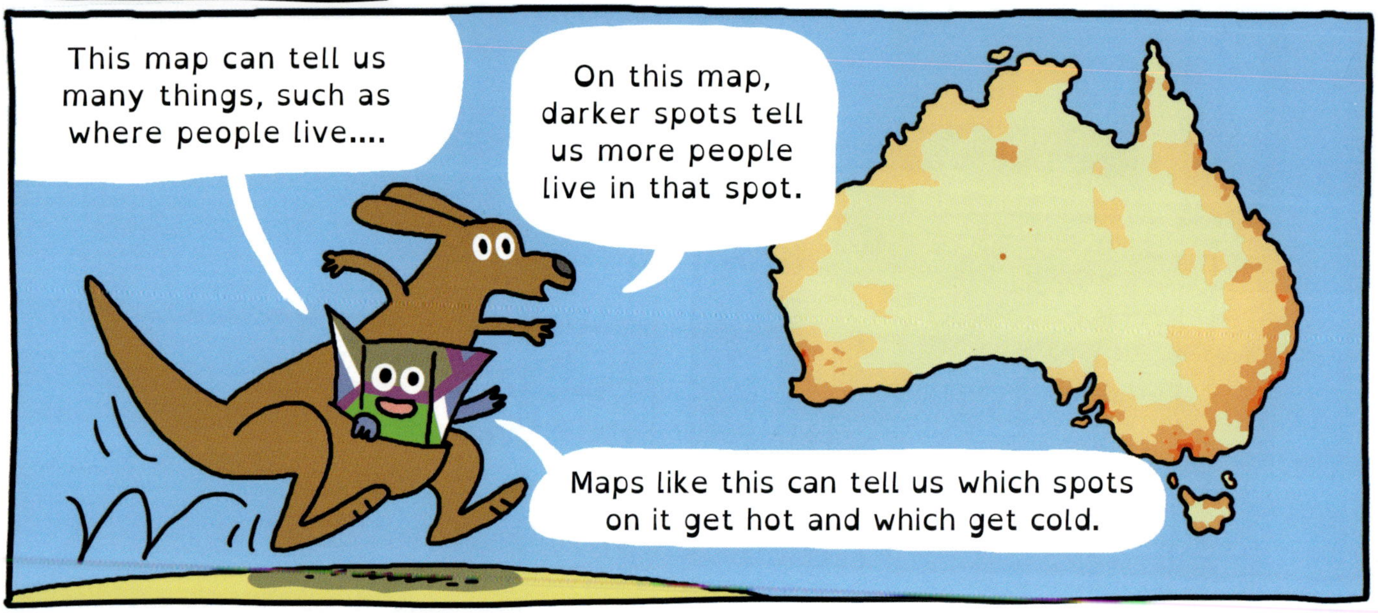
This map can tell us many things, such as where people live....
On this map, darker spots tell us more people live in that spot.
Maps like this can tell us which spots on it get hot and which get cold.

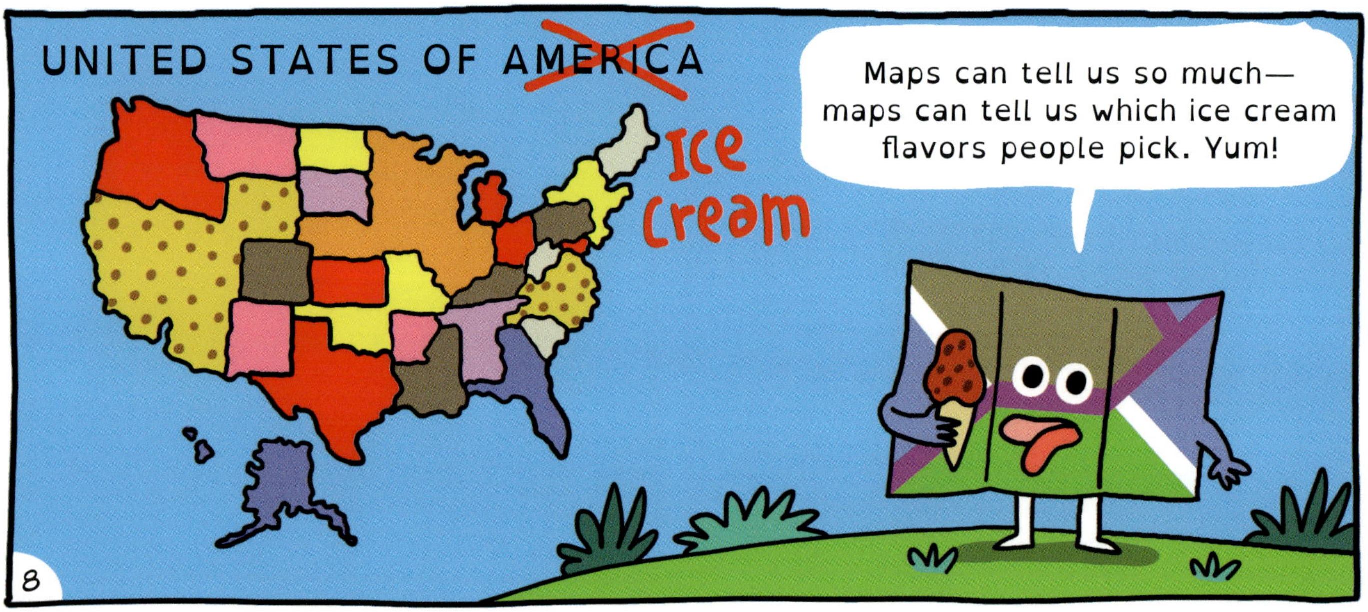
UNITED STATES OF AMERICA
Ice Cream
Maps can tell us so much—maps can tell us which ice cream flavors people pick. Yum!

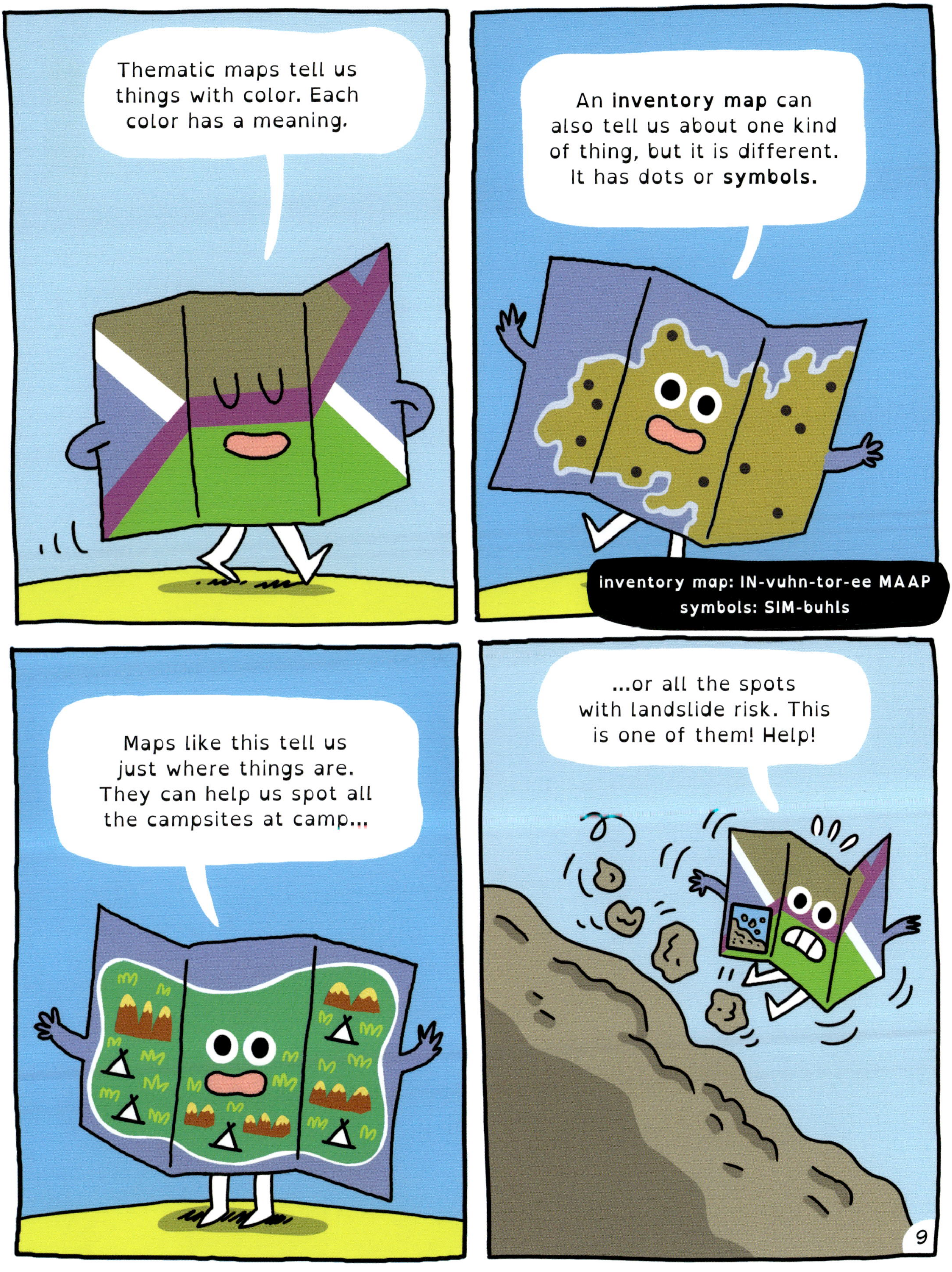
Thematic maps tell us things with color. Each color has a meaning.
An inventory map can also tell us about one kind of thing, but it is different. It has dots or symbols.
inventory map: IN-vuhn-tor-ee MAAP
symbols: SIM-buhls
Maps like this tell us just where things are. They can help us spot all the campsites at camp...
...or all the spots with landslide risk. This is one of them! Help!

MAP SCALES

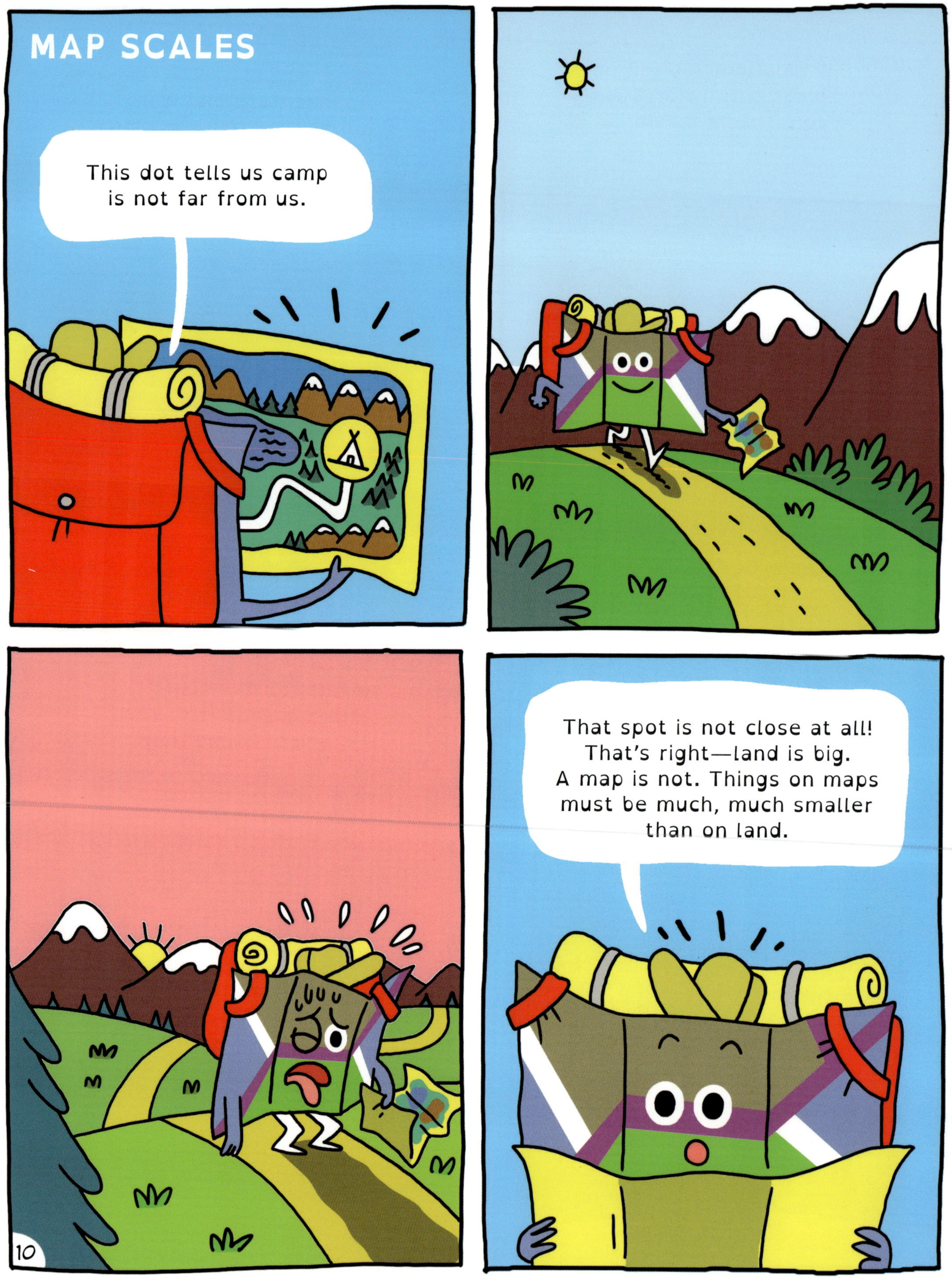
This dot tells us camp is not far from us.
That spot is not close at all! That's right—land is big. A map is not. Things on maps must be much, much smaller than on land.

How much smaller are things on maps? Maps tell us that! Most maps have a scale on them. This scale lets us compare land size and map size.
0 150 300 KM
0 50 200 MILES
A map scale tells us how big that map must be to match how big land is.
1 inch (2.5 centimeters) on this map is the same as 10 miles (16 kilometers) on land.
Map scales can be very different on different maps. This map is of Earth. It is a small-scale map. An inch (centimeter) on this map stands for lots of miles (kilometers) on land.
Small-scale maps tell us about big things. They do not show small things. A dot can stand for a whole city. That map will not tell us about buildings or streets.

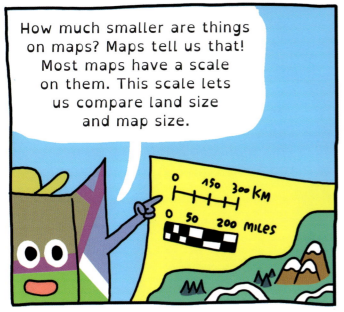

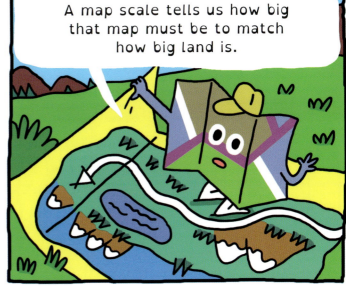

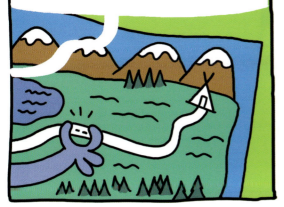

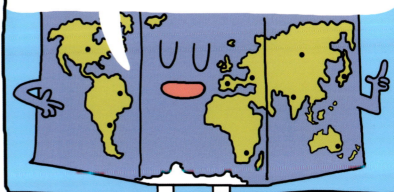

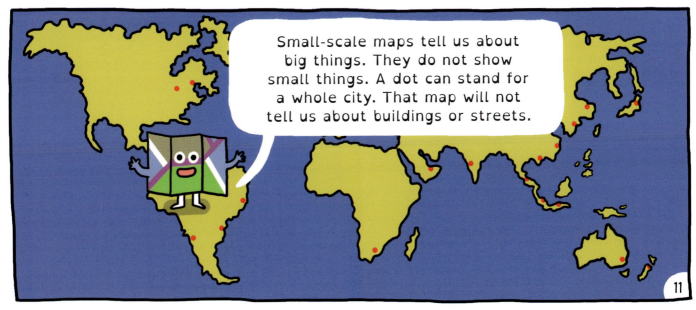

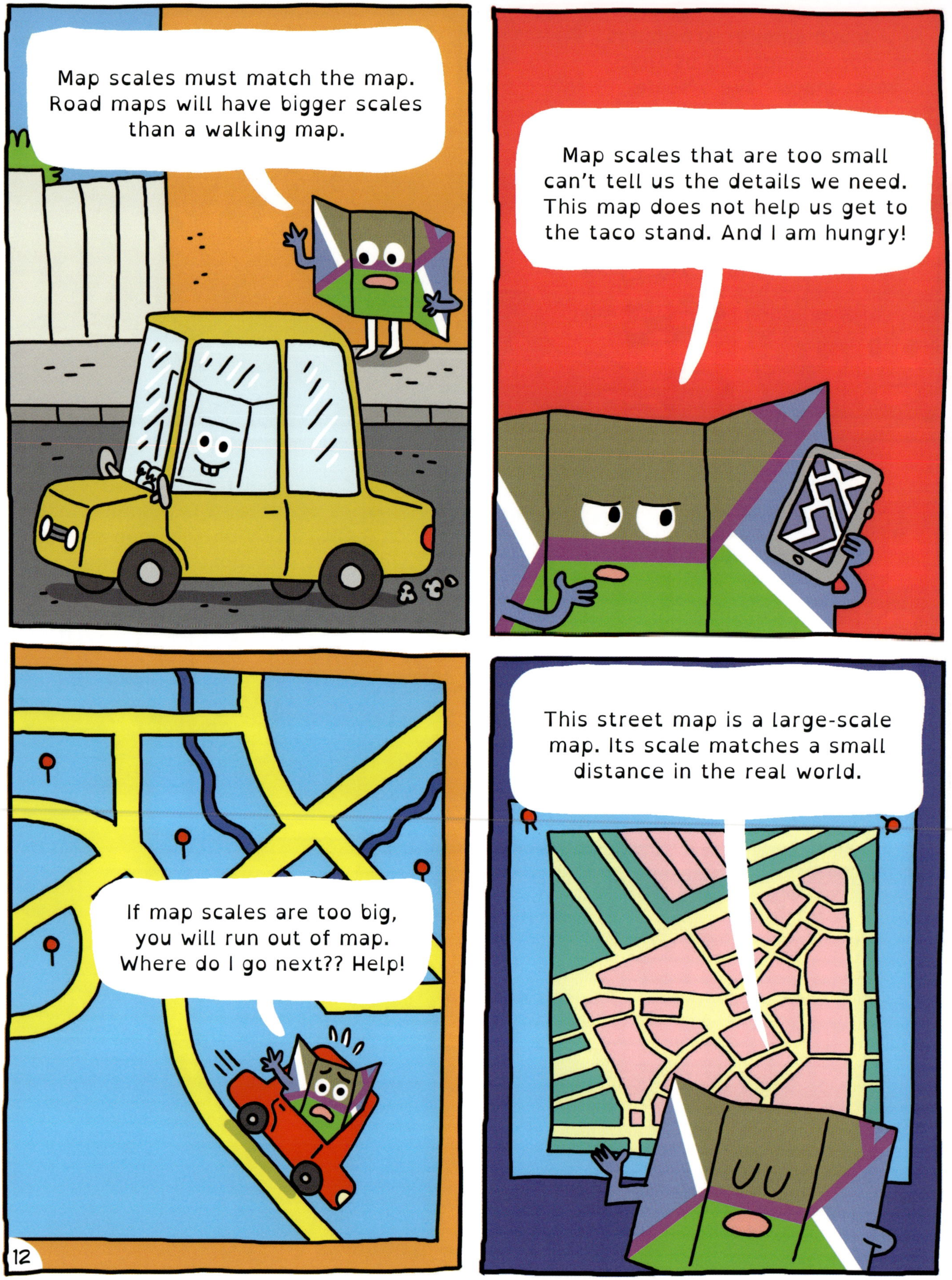
Map scales must match the map. Road maps will have bigger scales than a walking map.
Map scales that are too small can't tell us the details we need. This map does not help us get to the taco stand. And I am hungry!
If map scales are too big, you will run out of map. Where do I go next?? Help!
This street map is a large-scale map. Its scale matches a small distance in the real world.

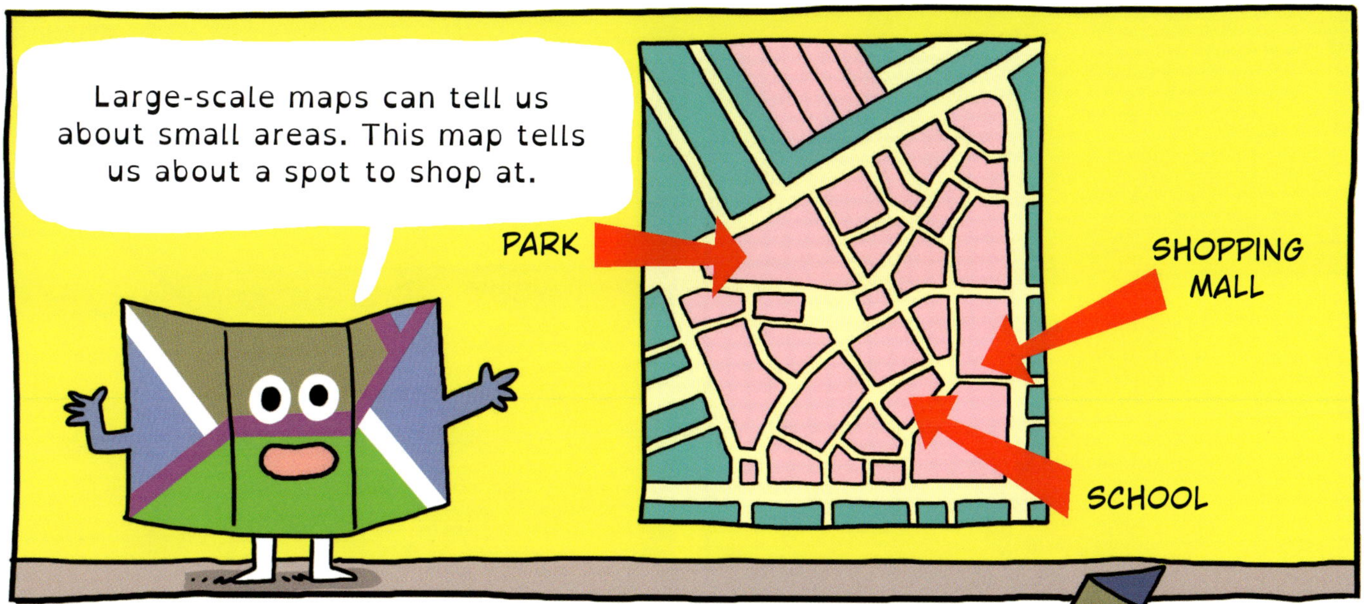
Large-scale maps can tell us about small areas. This map tells us about a spot to shop at.
PARK
SHOPPING MALL
SCHOOL

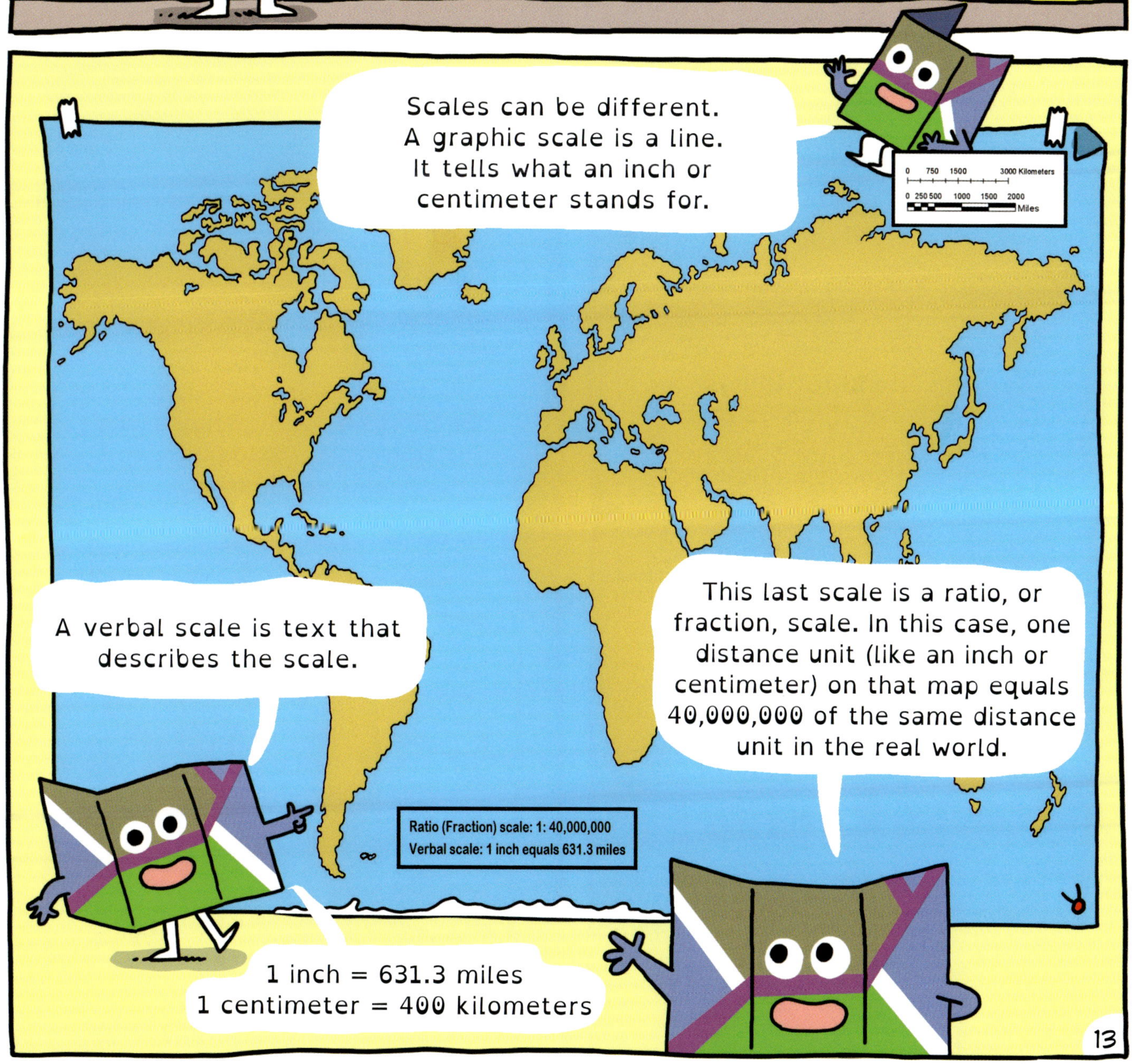
Scales can be different. A graphic scale is a line. It tells what an inch or centimeter stands for.
0 750 1500 3000 Kilometers
0 250 500 1000 1500 2000 Miles
A verbal scale is text that describes the scale.
1 inch = 631.3 miles
1 centimeter = 400 kilometers
Ratio (Fraction) scale: 1: 40,000,000
Verbal scale: 1 inch equals 631.3 miles
This last scale is a ratio, or fraction, scale. In this case, one distance unit (like an inch or centimeter) on that map equals 40,000,000 of the same distance unit in the real world.

MAP SYMBOLS AND LEGENDS

This tree is on my map. Will it be on this path?
It will not. It is just a symbol. It stands for a forest.
Symbols stand for things. Map makers use them on maps. This helps us read maps. It tells us a lot with just this small symbol.
PICNIC
BIKE PATH
BUS STOP
BUS STOP
HOSPITAL
LIBRARY
Lines on maps tell us lots of things as well. They stand for things like roads, streams, and **boundaries.**
RIVER
PROPOSED ROAD
BRIDGE
TOLL
HOUSING WITH NUMBER BESIDE ROAD
LIGHT RAIL & STATION
TRAIN RAIL & STATION
STATE BOUNDARY
CITY BOUNDARY

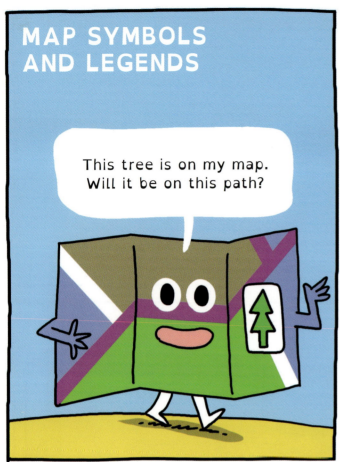

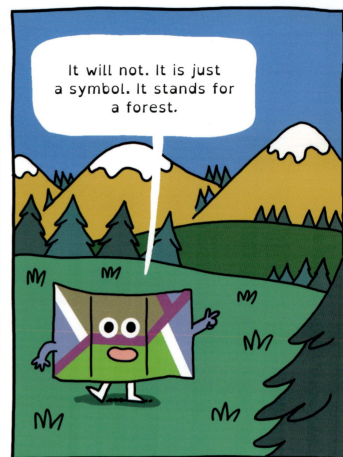

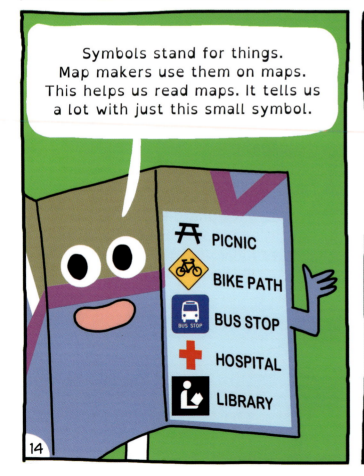

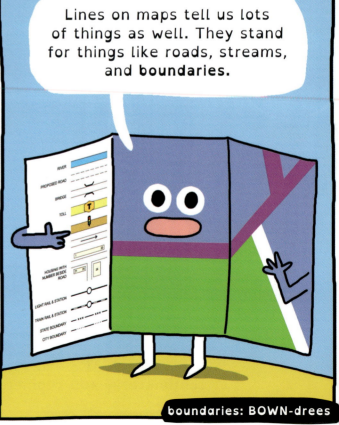

boundaries: BOWN-drees

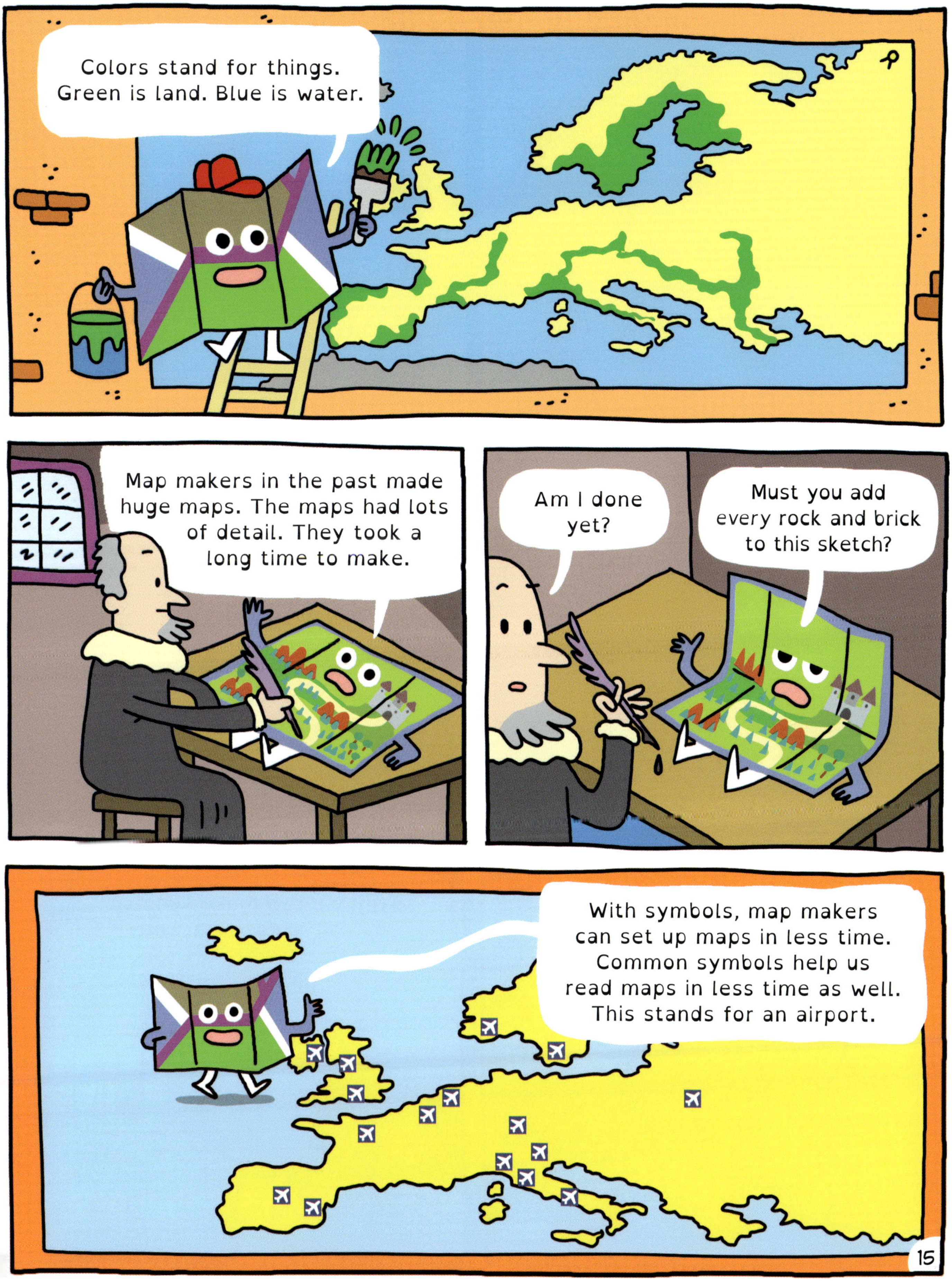

Colors stand for things. Green is land. Blue is water.
Map makers in the past made huge maps. The maps had lots of detail. They took a long time to make.
Am I done yet?
Must you add every rock and brick to this sketch?
With symbols, map makers can set up maps in less time. Common symbols help us read maps in less time as well. This stands for an airport.

This stands for a capital city. Lots of maps use this symbol.
Colors can stand for numbers. Blue, gray, and white on this map tell us how likely it is that it will snow in that place on December 25th.
This spot had light shading!
Symbols can make sense. You can guess what they mean. This stands for a gas station.

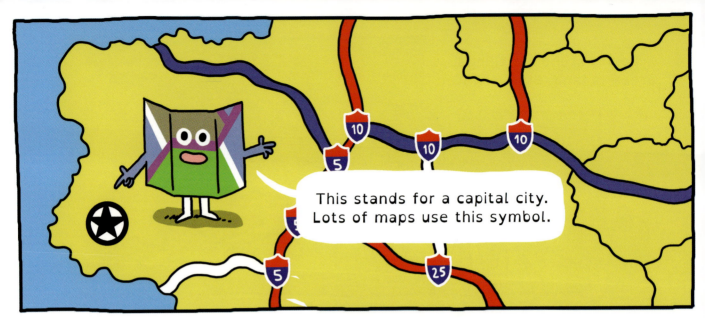

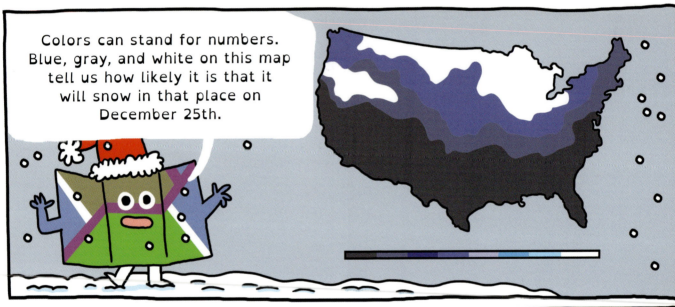

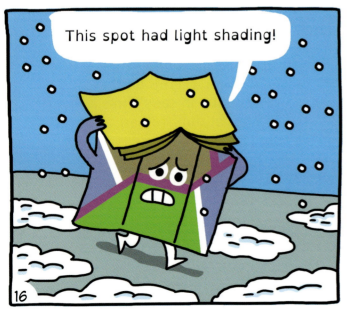

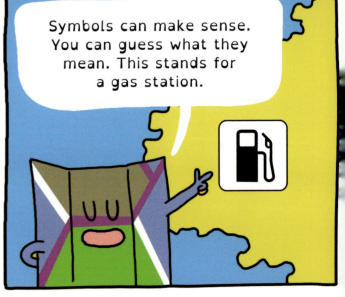

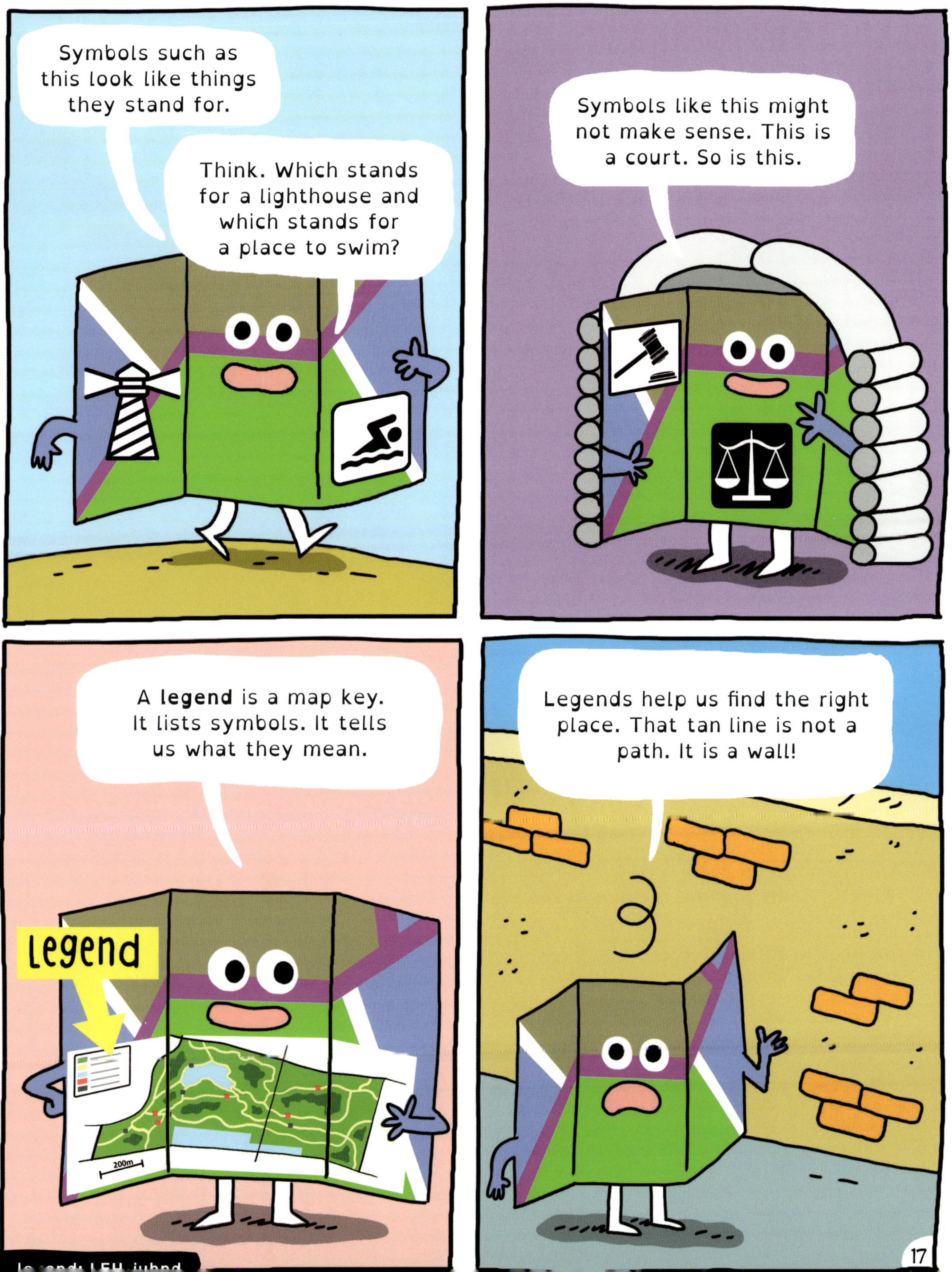
Symbols such as this look like things they stand for.
Think. Which stands for a lighthouse and which stands for a place to swim?
Symbols like this might not make sense. This is a court. So is this.
A **legend** is a map key. It lists symbols. It tells us what they mean.
Legend
200m
Legends help us find the right place. That tan line is not a path. It is a wall!

MAP COMPASS

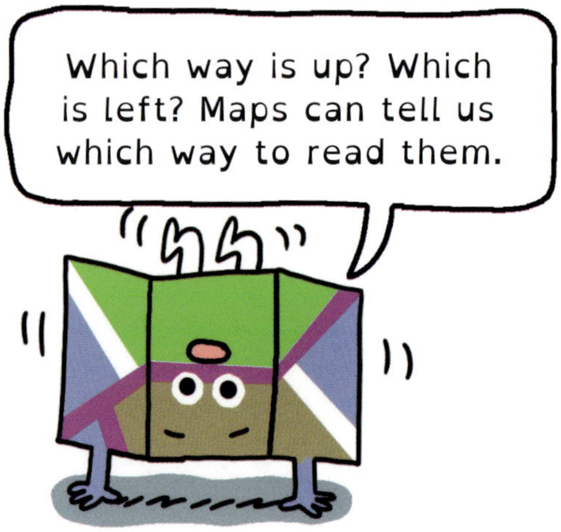
Which way is up? Which is left? Maps can tell us which way to read them.

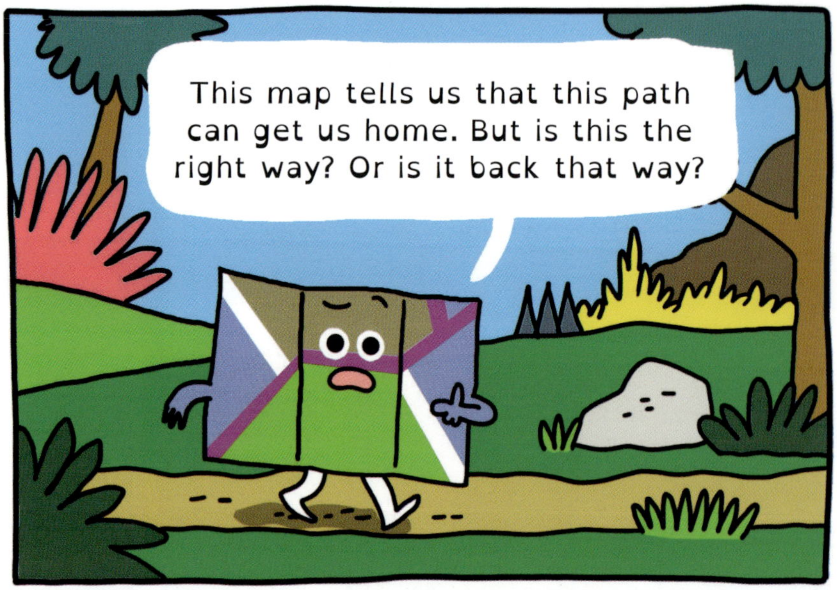
This map tells us that this path can get us home. But is this the right way? Or is it back that way?

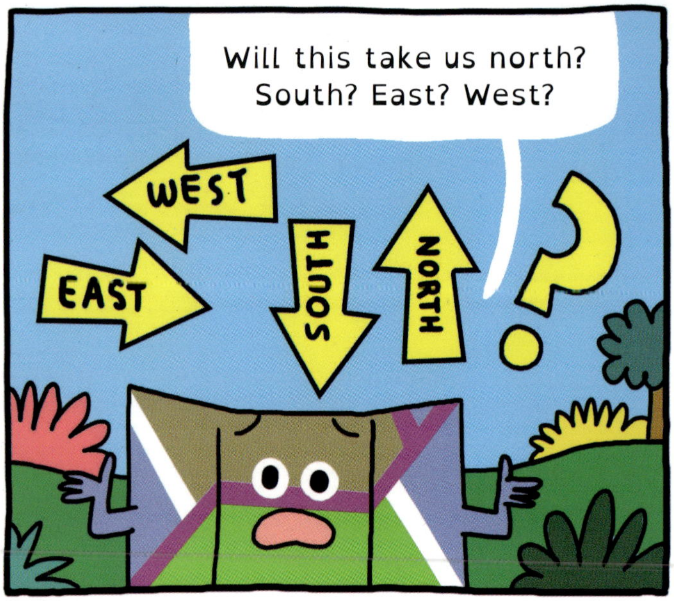
Will this take us north? South? East? West?
WEST
EAST
SOUTH
NORTH

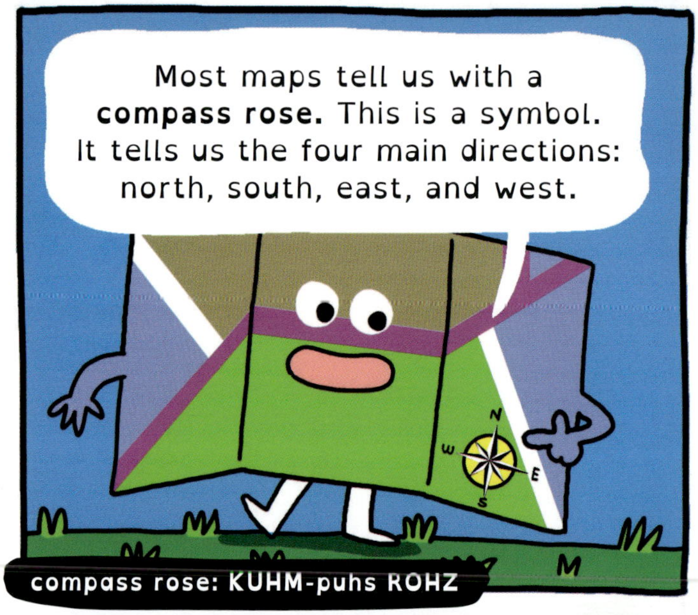
Most maps tell us with a **compass rose.** This is a symbol. It tells us the four main directions: north, south, east, and west.
compass rose: KUHM-puhs ROHZ

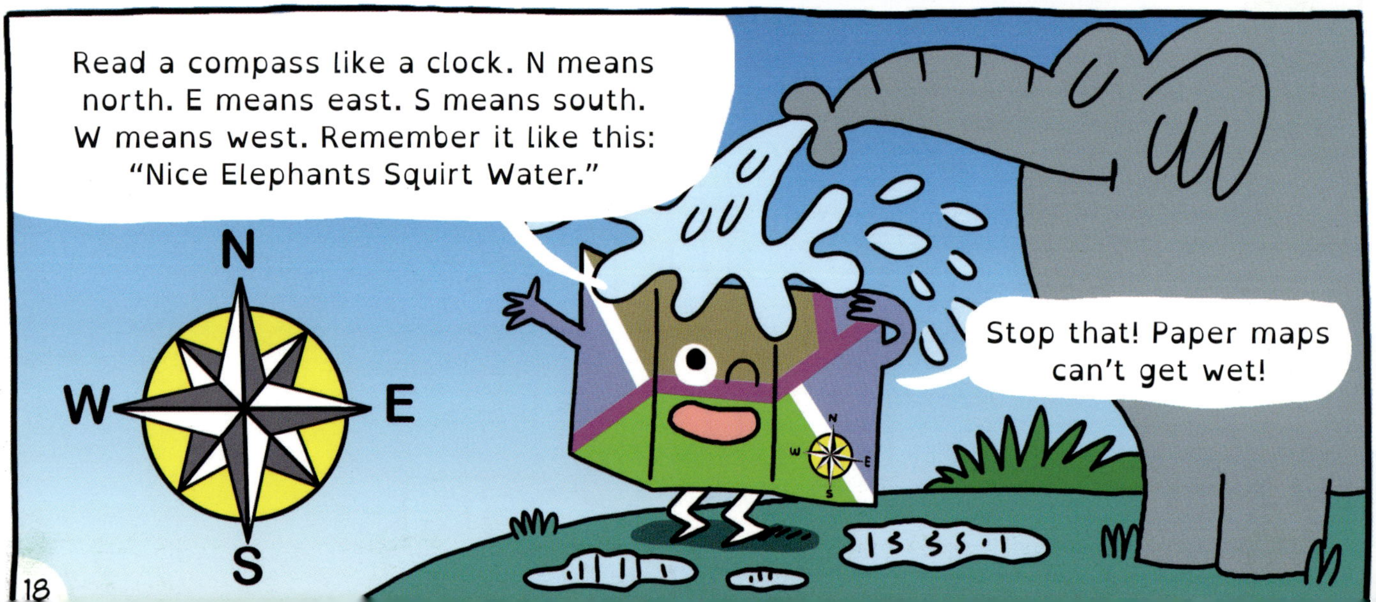
Read a compass like a clock. N means north. E means east. S means south. W means west. Remember it like this: "Nice Elephants Squirt Water."
N
W
E
S
Stop that! Paper maps can't get wet!

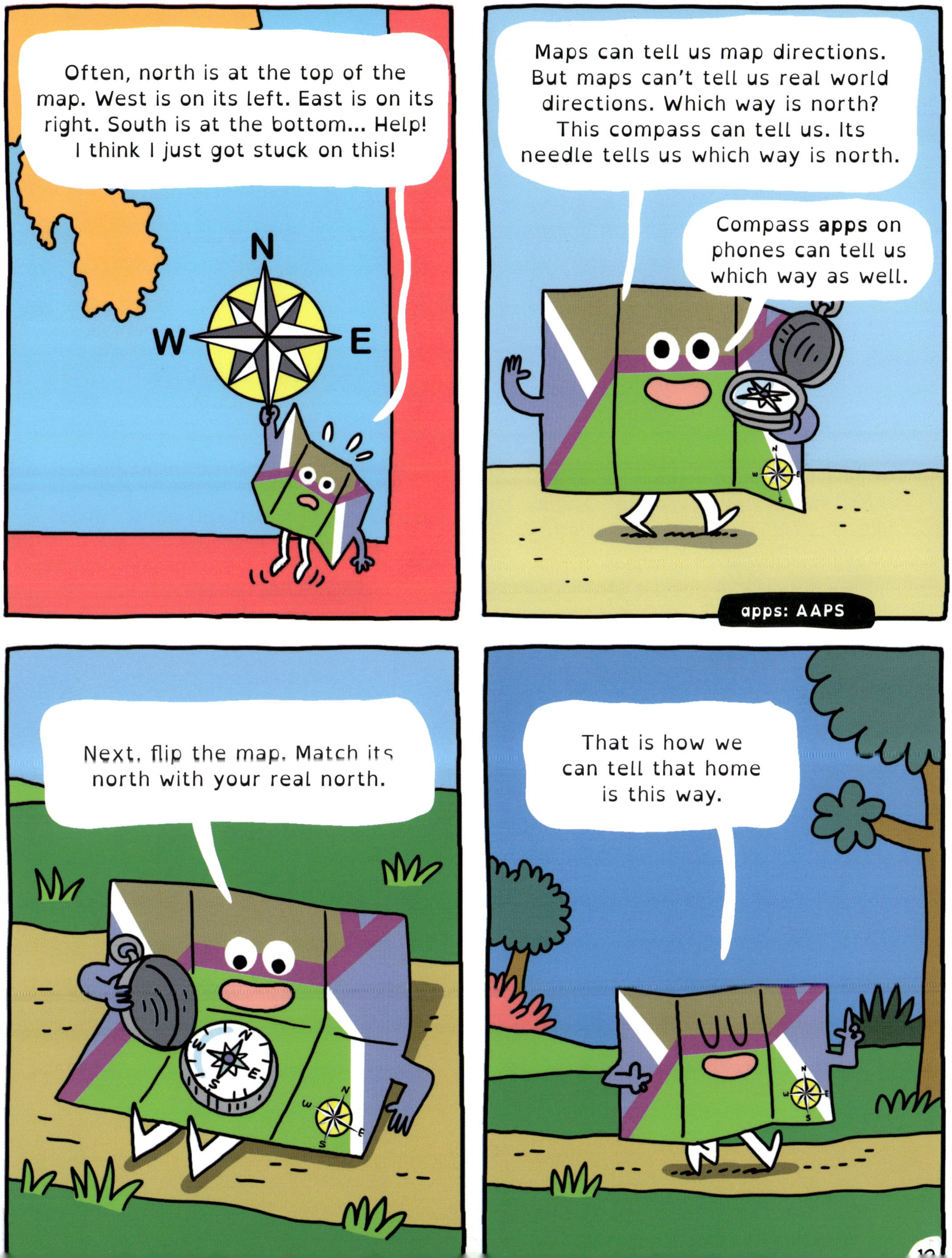
Often, north is at the top of the map. West is on its left. East is on its right. South is at the bottom... Help! I think I just got stuck on this!
N
W
E
Maps can tell us map directions. But maps can't tell us real world directions. Which way is north? This compass can tell us. Its needle tells us which way is north.
Compass **apps** on phones can tell us which way as well.
apps: AAPS
Next, flip the map. Match its north with your real north.
That is how we can tell that home is this way.

TOPOGRAPHIC MAPS

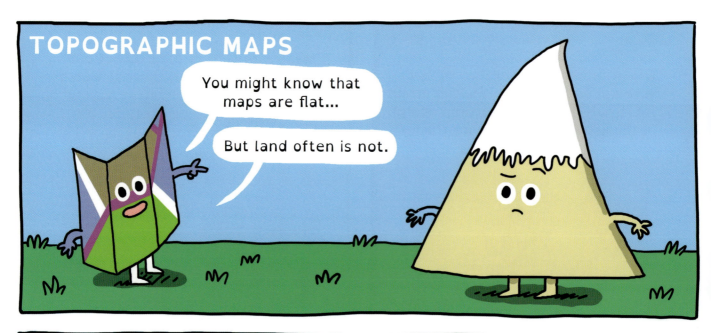

You might know that maps are flat...

But land often is not.

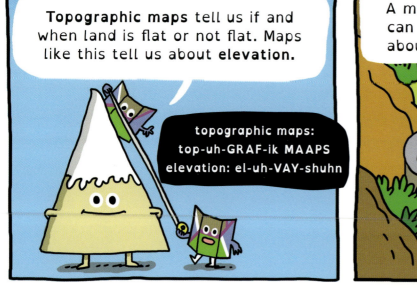

Topographic maps tell us if and when land is flat or not flat. Maps like this tell us about **elevation**.

topographic maps: top-uh-GRAF-ik MAAPS
elevation: el-uh-VAY-shuhn

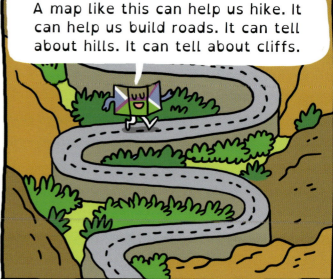

A map like this can help us hike. It can help us build roads. It can tell about hills. It can tell about cliffs.

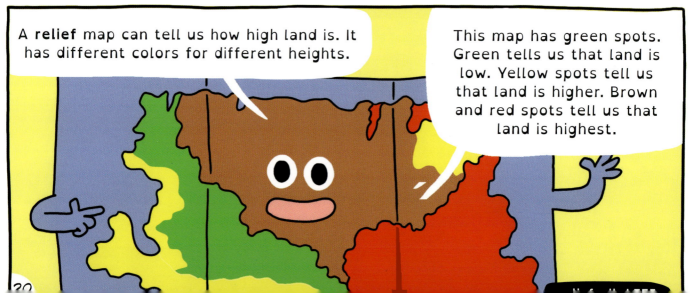

A **relief** map can tell us how high land is. It has different colors for different heights.

This map has green spots. Green tells us that land is low. Yellow spots tell us that land is higher. Brown and red spots tell us that land is highest.

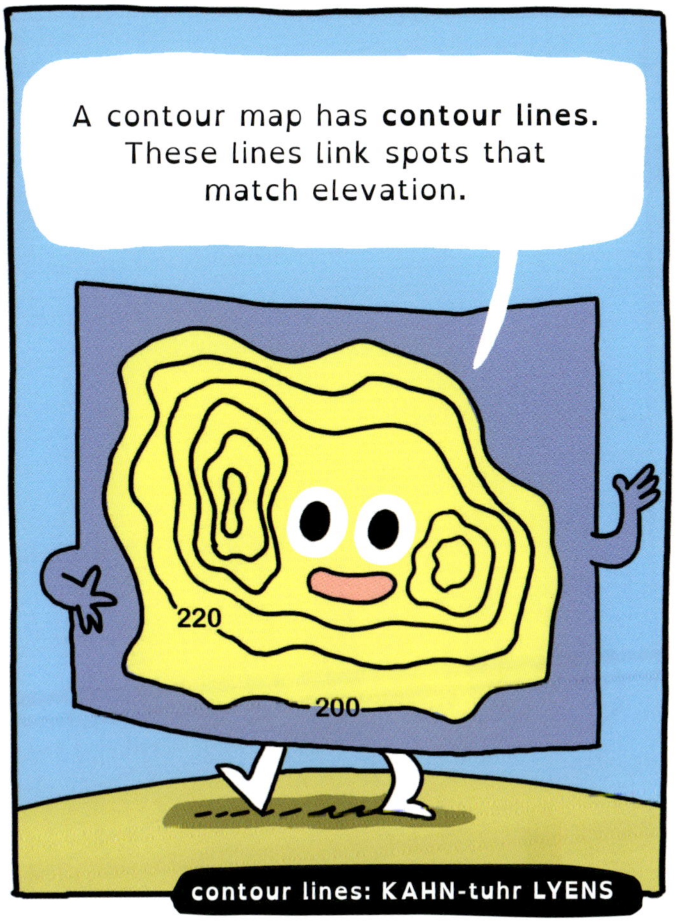
A contour map has **contour lines.** These lines link spots that match elevation.
220
200
contour lines: KAHN-tuhr LYENS

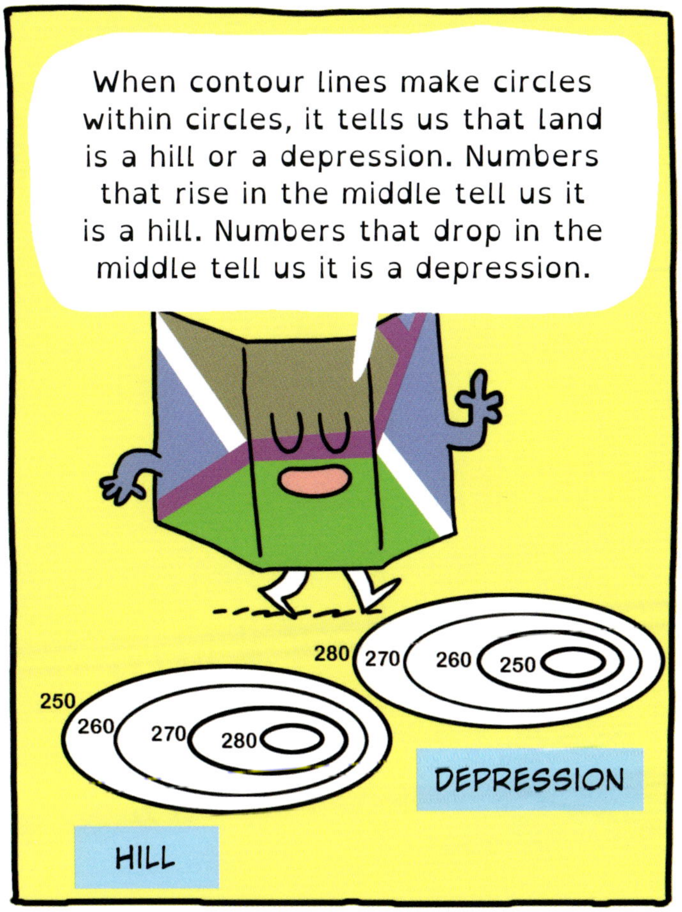
When contour lines make circles within circles, it tells us that land is a hill or a depression. Numbers that rise in the middle tell us it is a hill. Numbers that drop in the middle tell us it is a depression.
280 270 260 250
250 260 270 280
DEPRESSION
HILL

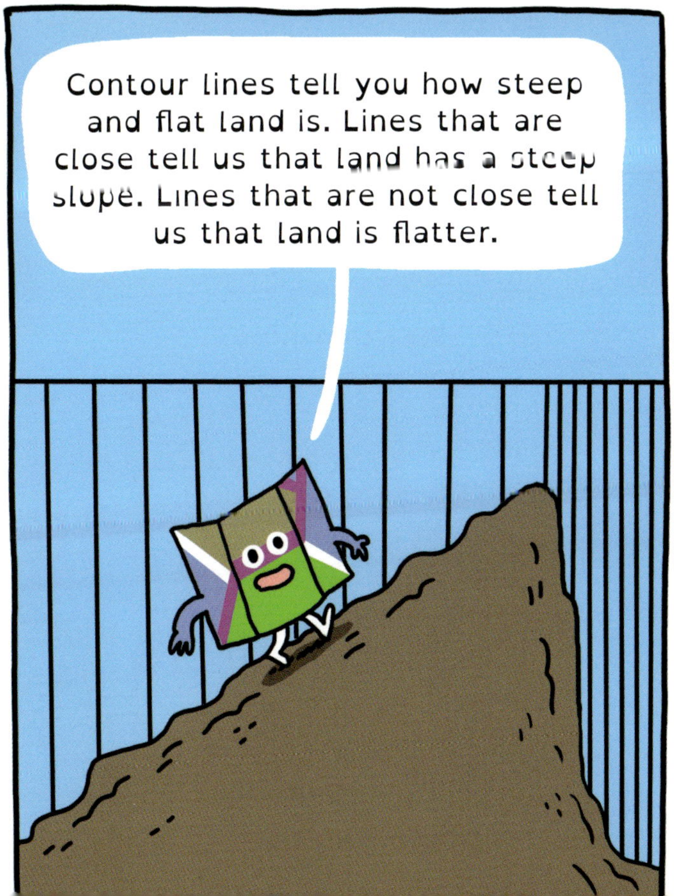
Contour lines tell you how steep and flat land is. Lines that are close tell us that land has a steep slope. Lines that are not close tell us that land is flatter.

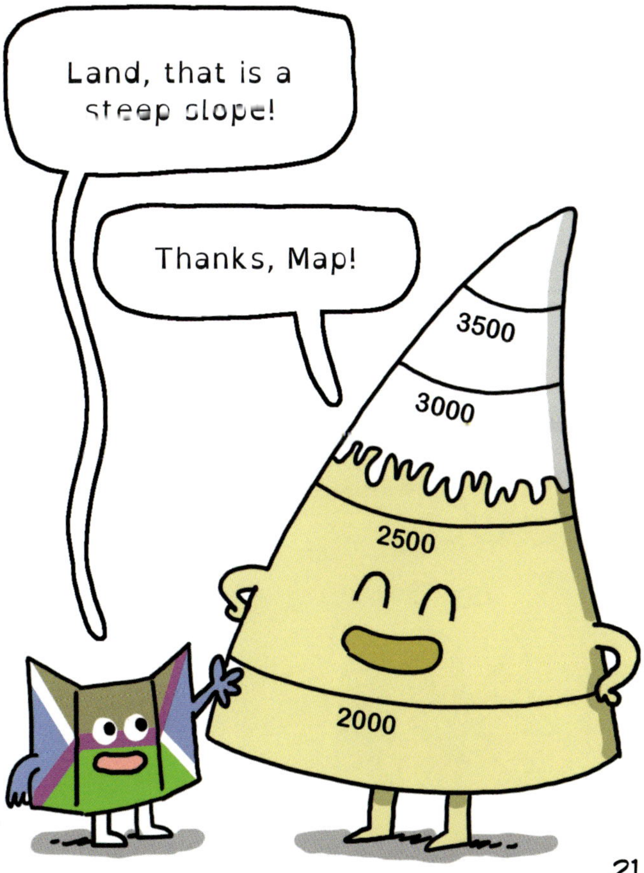
Land, that is a steep slope!
Thanks, Map!
3500
3000
2500
2000

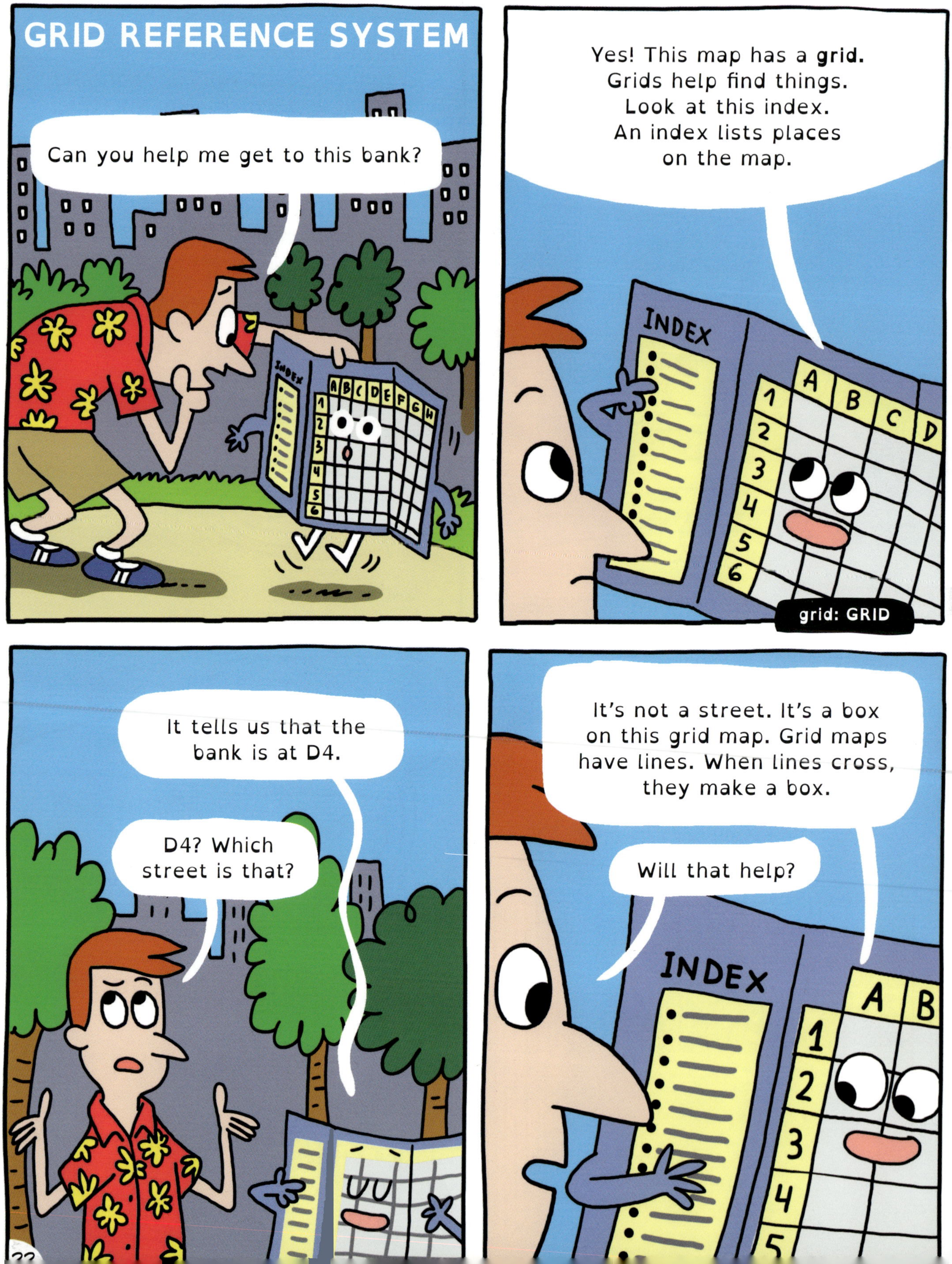
GRID REFERENCE SYSTEM
Can you help me get to this bank?
INDEX
A B C D E F G H
1 2 3 4 5 6
Yes! This map has a **grid.** Grids help find things. Look at this index. An index lists places on the map.
INDEX
A B C D
1 2 3 4 5 6
grid: GRID
It tells us that the bank is at D4.
D4? Which street is that?
It's not a street. It's a box on this grid map. Grid maps have lines. When lines cross, they make a box.
Will that help?
INDEX
A B
1 2 3 4 5

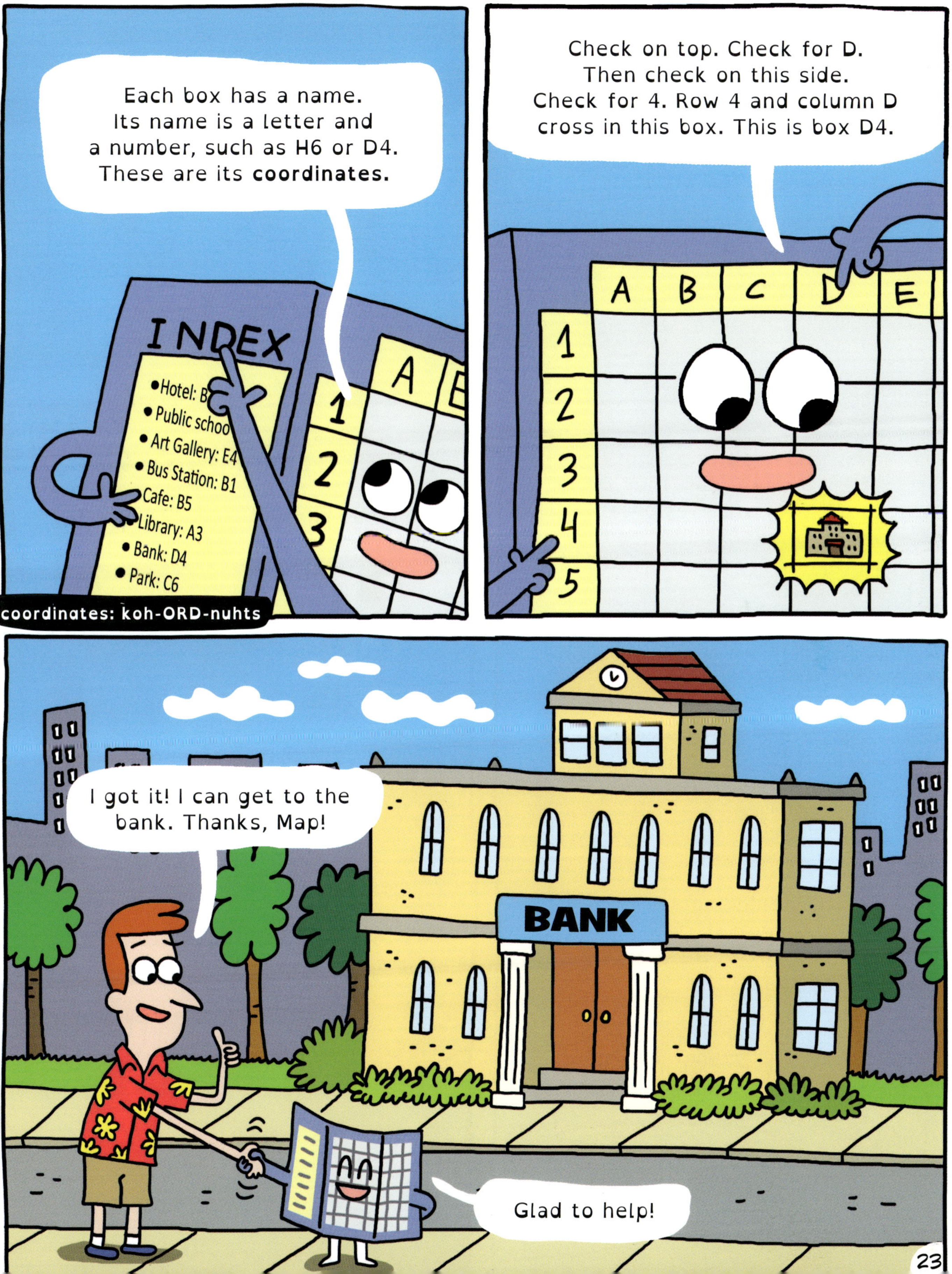
Each box has a name. Its name is a letter and a number, such as H6 or D4. These are its **coordinates.**
INDEX
Art Gallery: E4
Bus Station: B1
Cafe: B5
Library: A3
Bank: D4
Park: C6
coordinates: koh-ORD-nuhts
Check on top. Check for D. Then check on this side. Check for 4. Row 4 and column D cross in this box. This is box D4.
A B C D E
1 2 3 4 5
I got it! I can get to the bank. Thanks, Map!
BANK
Glad to help!

LATITUDE AND LONGITUDE
When small-scale maps show a lot of land, this big grid helps. Its name is the **graticule.**
This grid helps find an exact spot on Earth.
graticule: GRAA-tuh-kyool
This grid has two sets of lines. They are not real. They circle Earth. They are lines of **latitude** and **longitude**... Can I see them? Nope! They are definitely not real.
latitude: LAT-uh-tood longitude: LAWN-juh-tood
Latitude lines run east and west on each side of the **equator.** They are known as **parallels,** too. They tell us how far north or south a place is.
equator: ih-KWAY-tuhr
parallels: PAIR-uh-lelz
Latitude lines get smaller as you get farther north or south.
These lines are measured in degrees. Each degree is about 69 miles (111 kilometers). It does not look that far on this map!

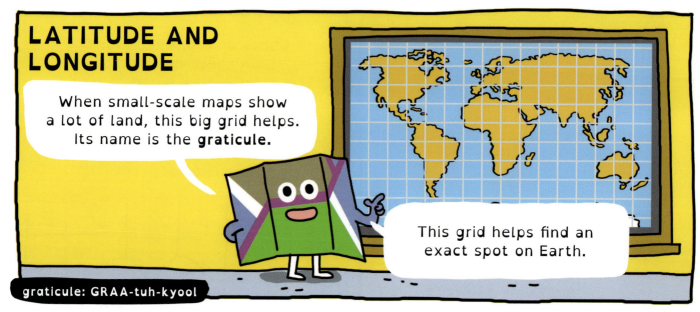

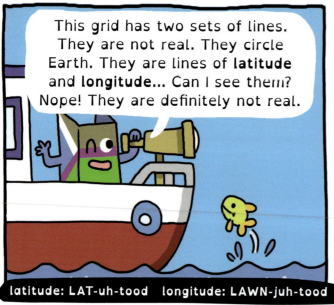

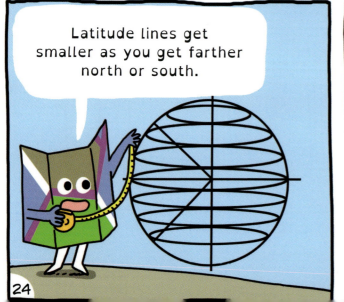

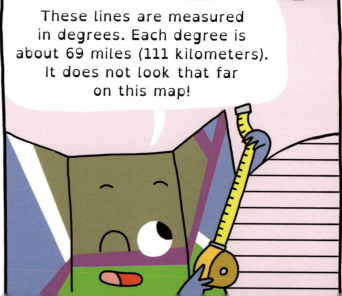

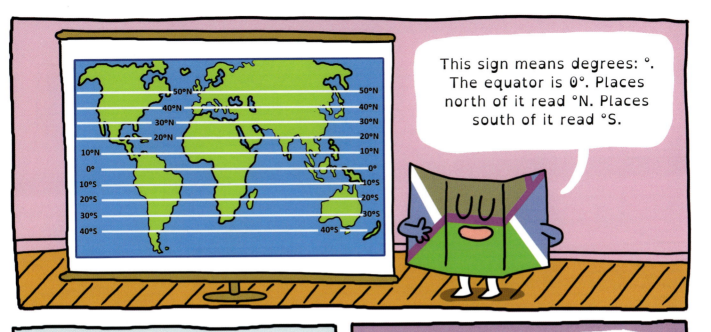

This sign means degrees: °. The equator is 0°. Places north of it read °N. Places south of it read °S.

This is cold! This is the North Pole. It is as far north as you can get. Its latitude is 90°N. The South Pole is 90°S. That is as far south as you can get. Let's get back to 0° latitude!

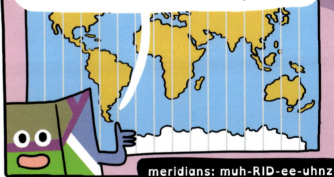

Longitude lines can also be known as **meridians.** They run north and south. They stretch from pole to pole. You can use these. You can tell how far east or west a place is.

meridians: muh-RID-ee-uhnz

Earth has 360 longitude lines. They are measured in degrees, too. At the equator, each line is 69 miles (111 kilometers) apart.

Earth is a sphere. Degrees of longitude shrink when they get close to the poles. They shrink to zero at the poles.

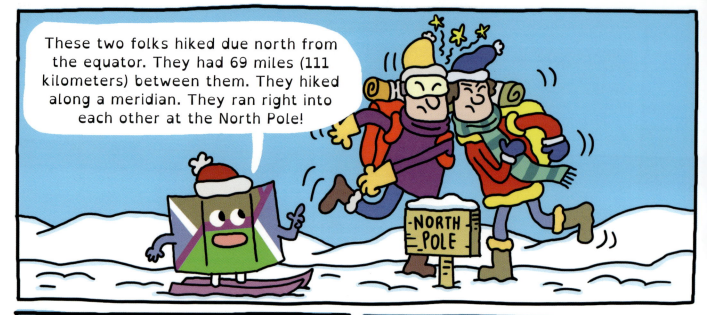

These two folks hiked due north from the equator. They had 69 miles (111 kilometers) between them. They hiked along a meridian. They ran right into each other at the North Pole!

Longitude lines begin at Greenwich in London, England. That is where the prime meridian is. It is 0° longitude.

Lines east of the prime meridian read °E. These make up the Eastern Hemisphere. Lines west of it read °W. These make up the Western Hemisphere.

These hemispheres meet on the other side of Earth. They meet on the 180th line. It goes through Taveuni, Fiji. It is an island.

This line is the International Date Line.

Latitude and longitude lines can find an exact spot on Earth. That spot is named with two numbers. These are its coordinates.

If you know a place's coordinates, you can find it!

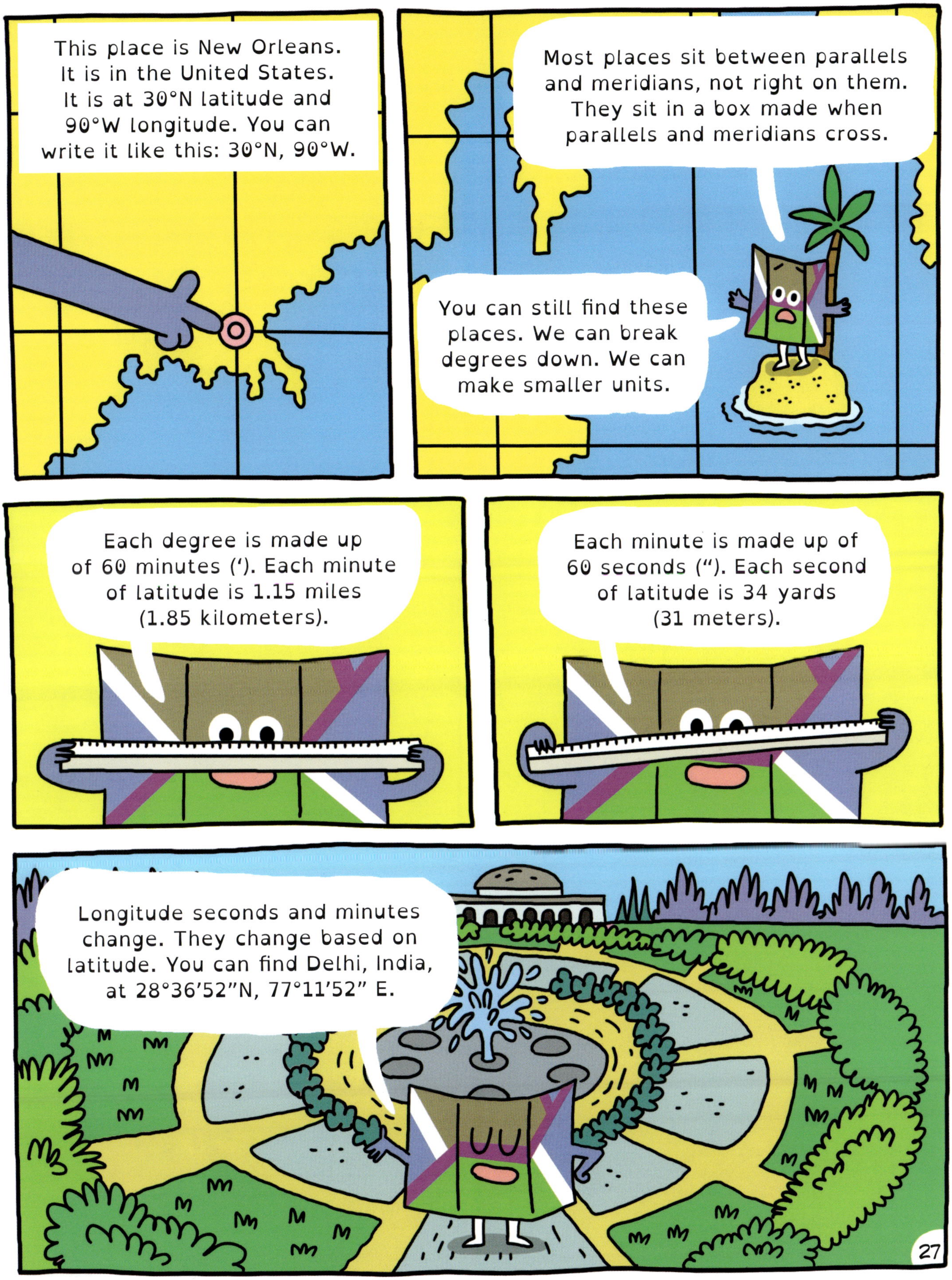

This place is New Orleans. It is in the United States. It is at 30°N latitude and 90°W longitude. You can write it like this: 30°N, 90°W.
Most places sit between parallels and meridians, not right on them. They sit in a box made when parallels and meridians cross.
You can still find these places. We can break degrees down. We can make smaller units.
Each degree is made up of 60 minutes (‘). Each minute of latitude is 1.15 miles (1.85 kilometers).
Each minute is made up of 60 seconds (“). Each second of latitude is 34 yards (31 meters).
Longitude seconds and minutes change. They change based on latitude. You can find Delhi, India, at 28°36’52”N, 77°11’52” E.

MAPS AND GLOBES

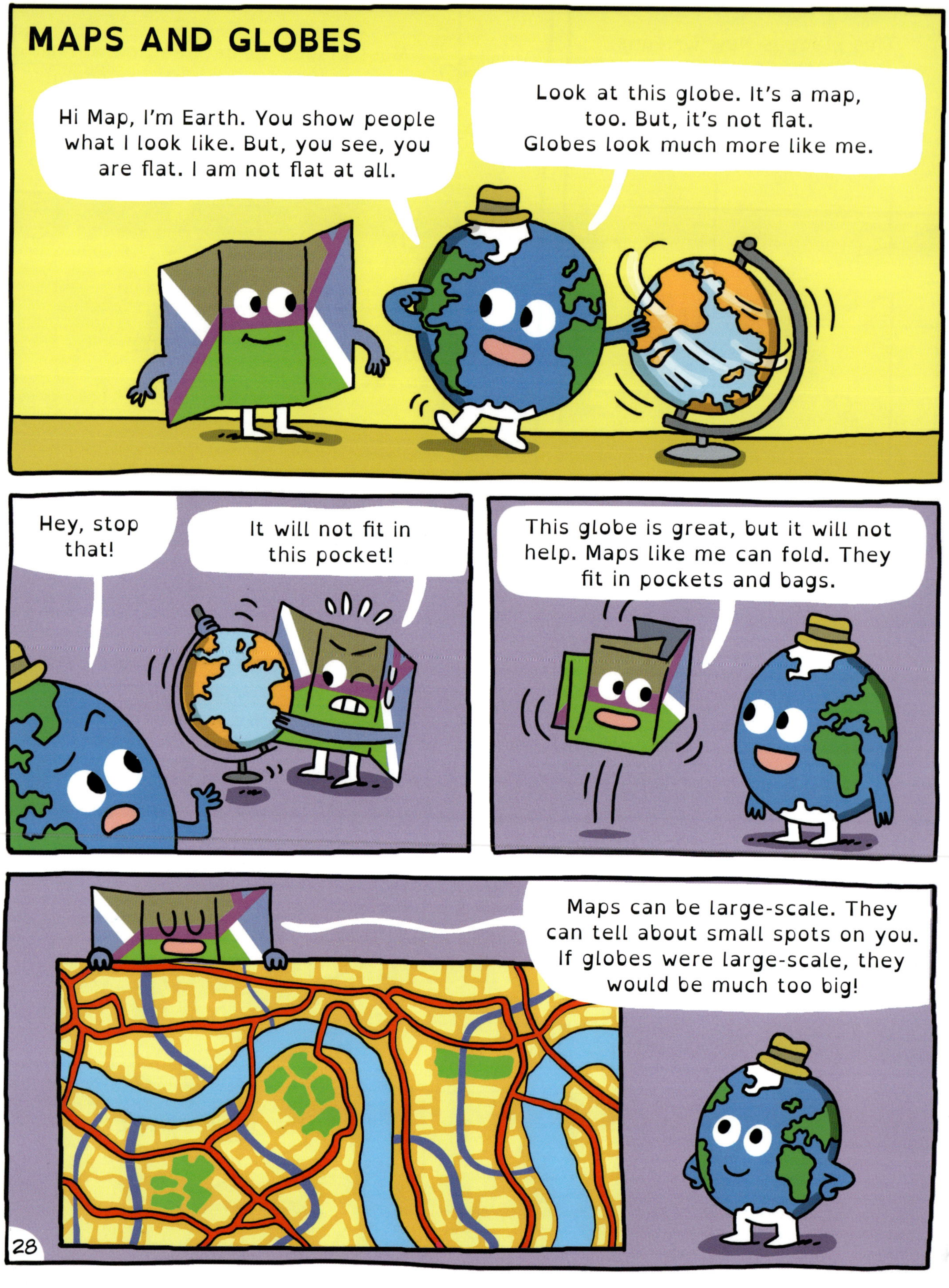
Hi Map, I'm Earth. You show people what I look like. But, you see, you are flat. I am not flat at all.
Look at this globe. It's a map, too. But, it's not flat. Globes look much more like me.
Hey, stop that!
It will not fit in this pocket!
This globe is great, but it will not help. Maps like me can fold. They fit in pockets and bags.
Maps can be large-scale. They can tell about small spots on you. If globes were large-scale, they would be much too big!

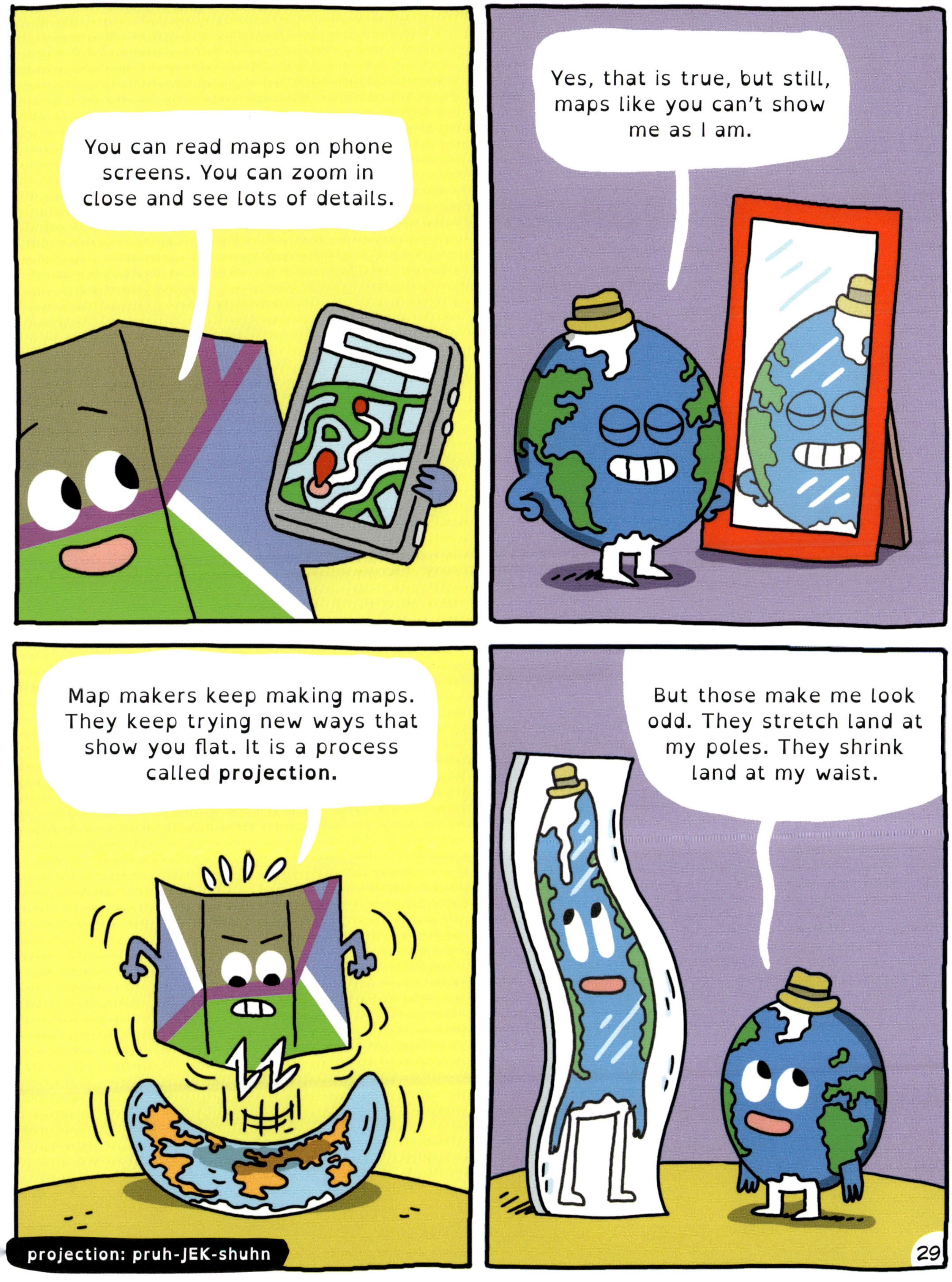
You can read maps on phone screens. You can zoom in close and see lots of details.
Yes, that is true, but still, maps like you can't show me as I am.
Map makers keep making maps. They keep trying new ways that show you flat. It is a process called **projection.**
But those make me look odd. They stretch land at my poles. They shrink land at my waist.
projection: pruh-JEK-shuhn

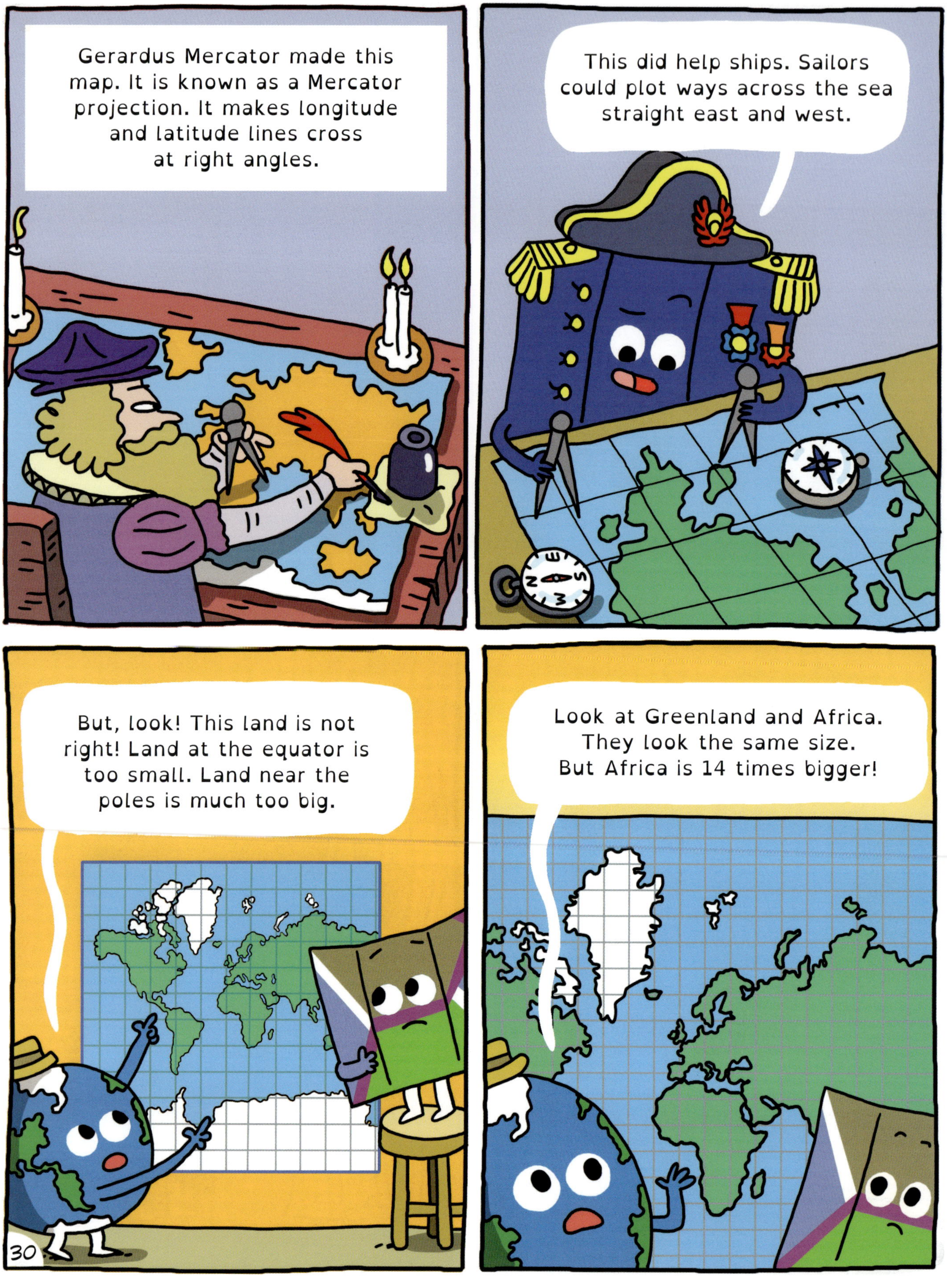
Gerardus Mercator made this map. It is known as a Mercator projection. It makes longitude and latitude lines cross at right angles.
This did help ships. Sailors could plot ways across the sea straight east and west.
E
N
E
S
W
But, look! This land is not right! Land at the equator is too small. Land near the poles is much too big.
Look at Greenland and Africa. They look the same size. But Africa is 14 times bigger!

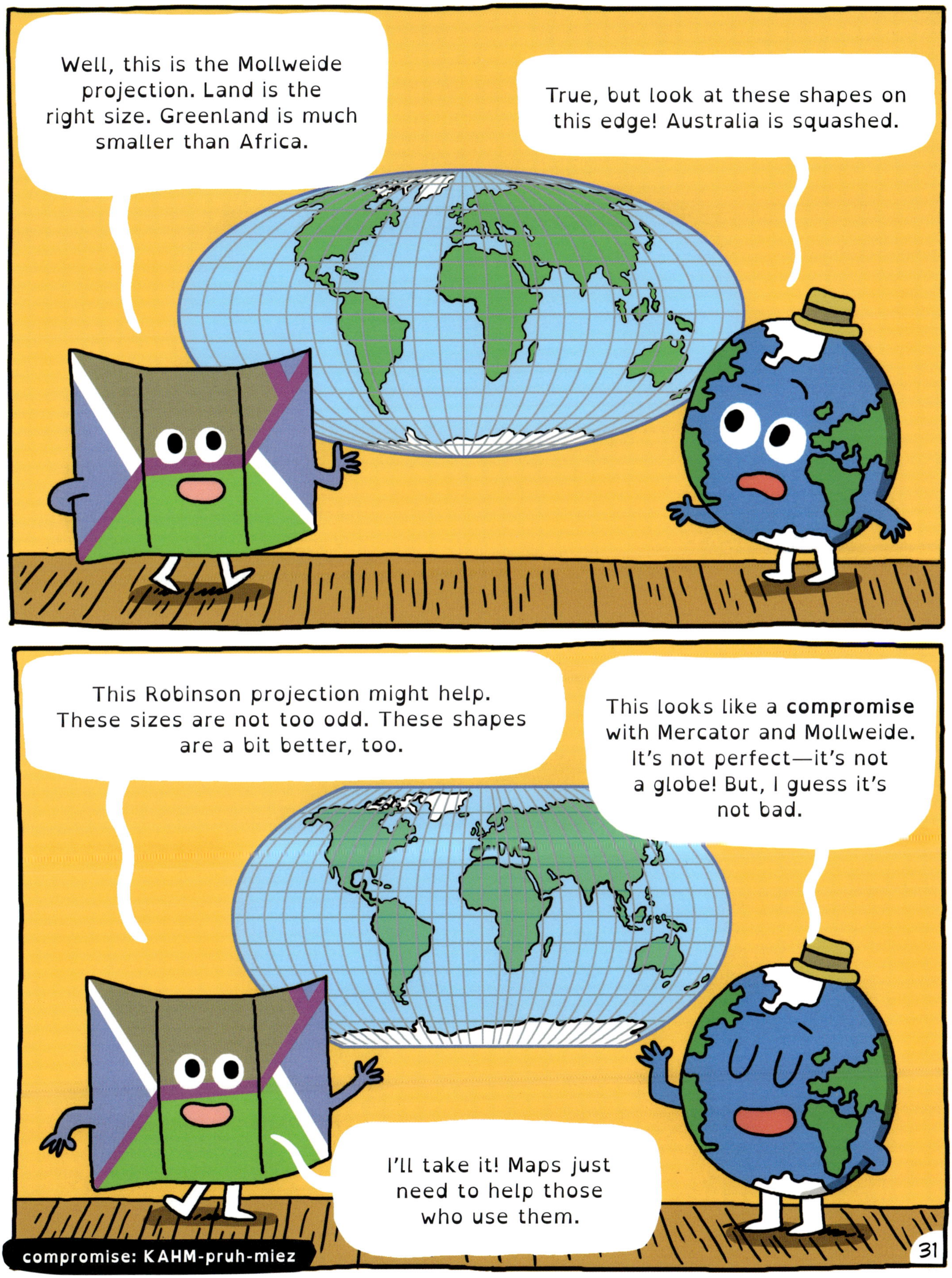

Well, this is the Mollweide projection. Land is the right size. Greenland is much smaller than Africa.
True, but look at these shapes on this edge! Australia is squashed.
This Robinson projection might help. These sizes are not too odd. These shapes are a bit better, too.
This looks like a **compromise** with Mercator and Mollweide. It's not perfect—it's not a globe! But, I guess it's not bad.
I'll take it! Maps just need to help those who use them.
compromise: KAHM-pruh-miez

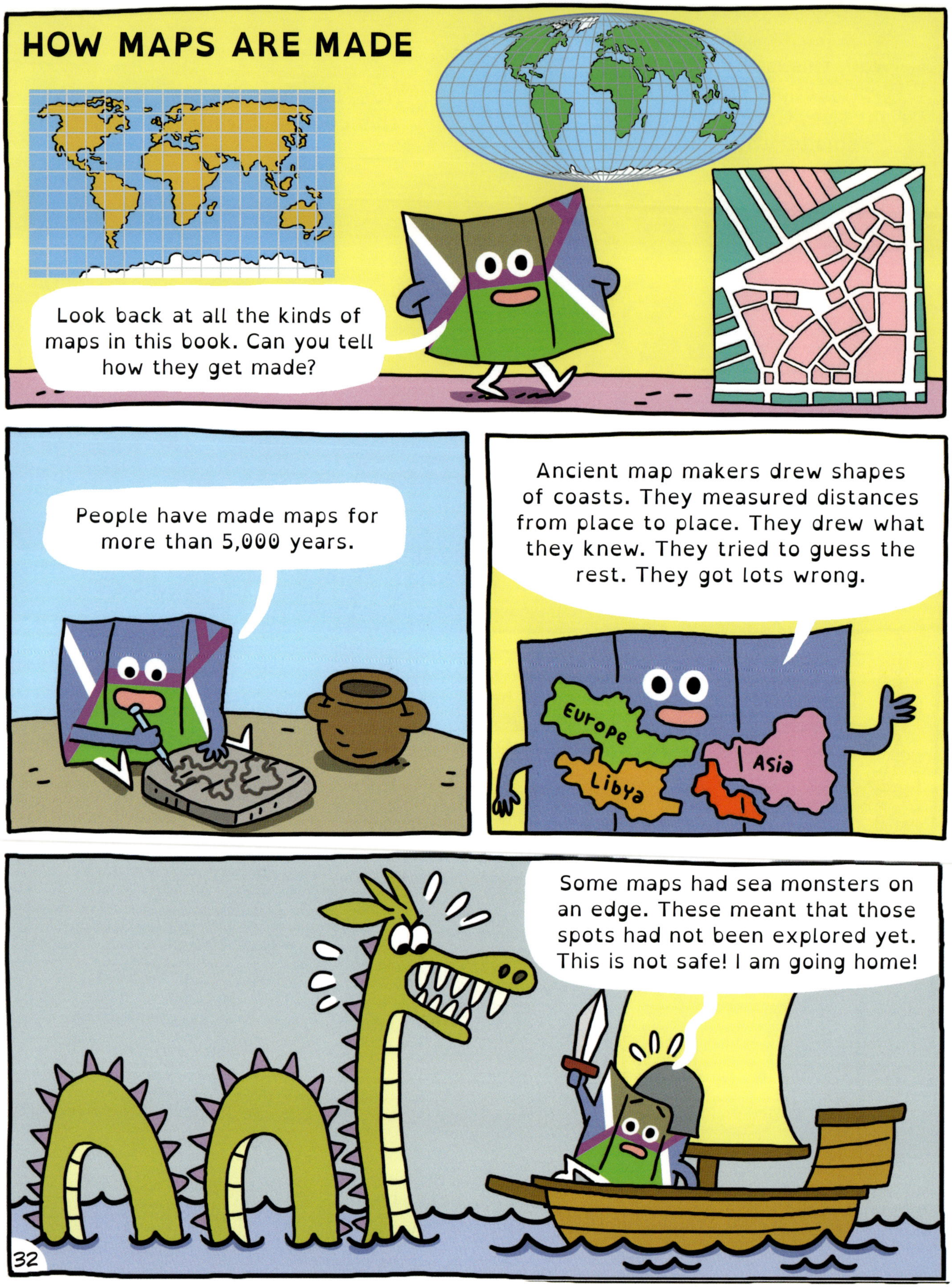
HOW MAPS ARE MADE
Look back at all the kinds of maps in this book. Can you tell how they get made?
People have made maps for more than 5,000 years.
Ancient map makers drew shapes of coasts. They measured distances from place to place. They drew what they knew. They tried to guess the rest. They got lots wrong.
Europe
Libya
Asia
Some maps had sea monsters on an edge. These meant that those spots had not been explored yet. This is not safe! I am going home!

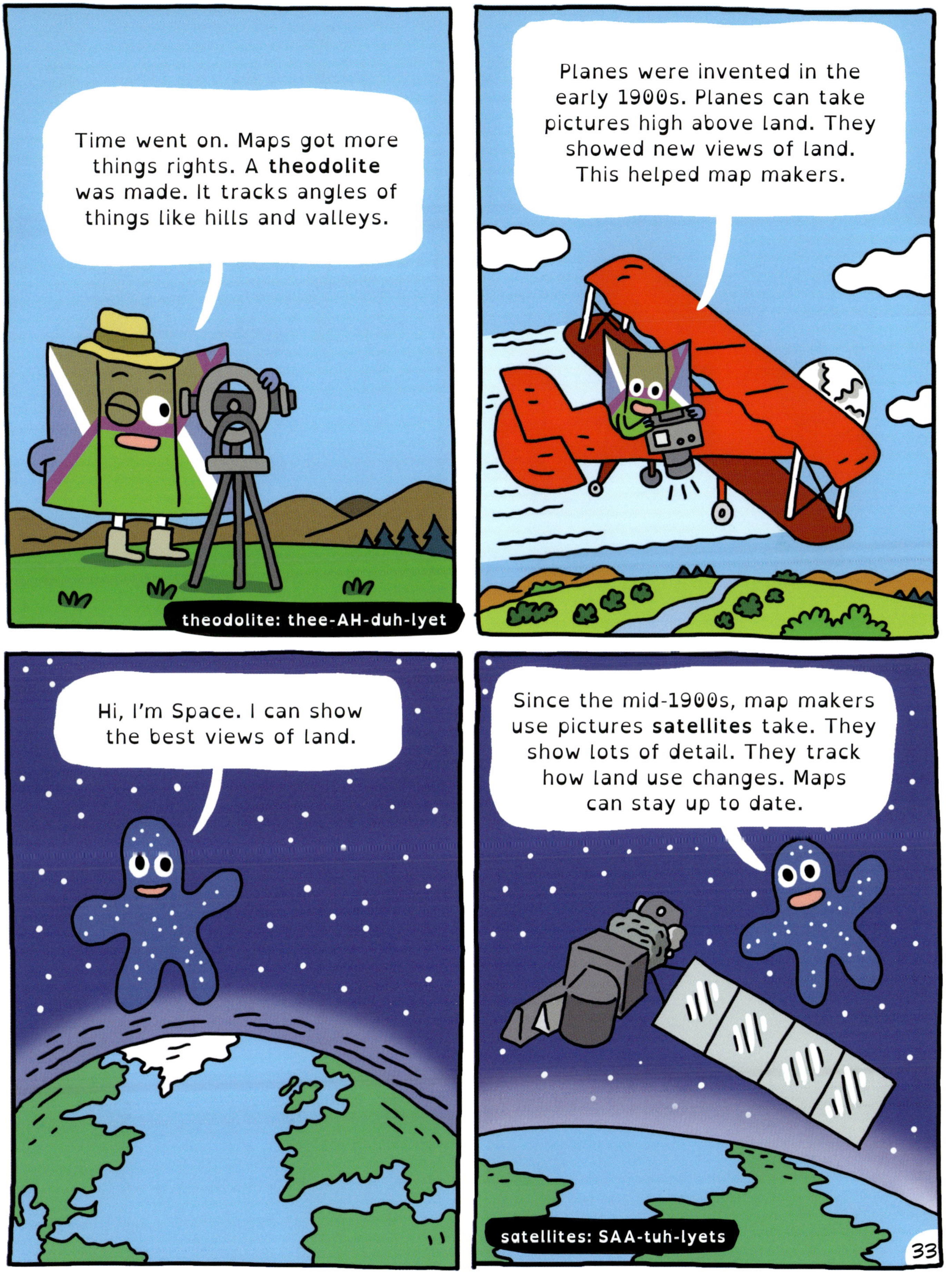
Time went on. Maps got more things rights. A **theodolite** was made. It tracks angles of things like hills and valleys.
theodolite: thee-AH-duh-lyet
Planes were invented in the early 1900s. Planes can take pictures high above land. They showed new views of land. This helped map makers.
Hi, I'm Space. I can show the best views of land.
Since the mid-1900s, map makers use pictures **satellites** take. They show lots of detail. They track how land use changes. Maps can stay up to date.
satellites: SAA-tuh-lyets

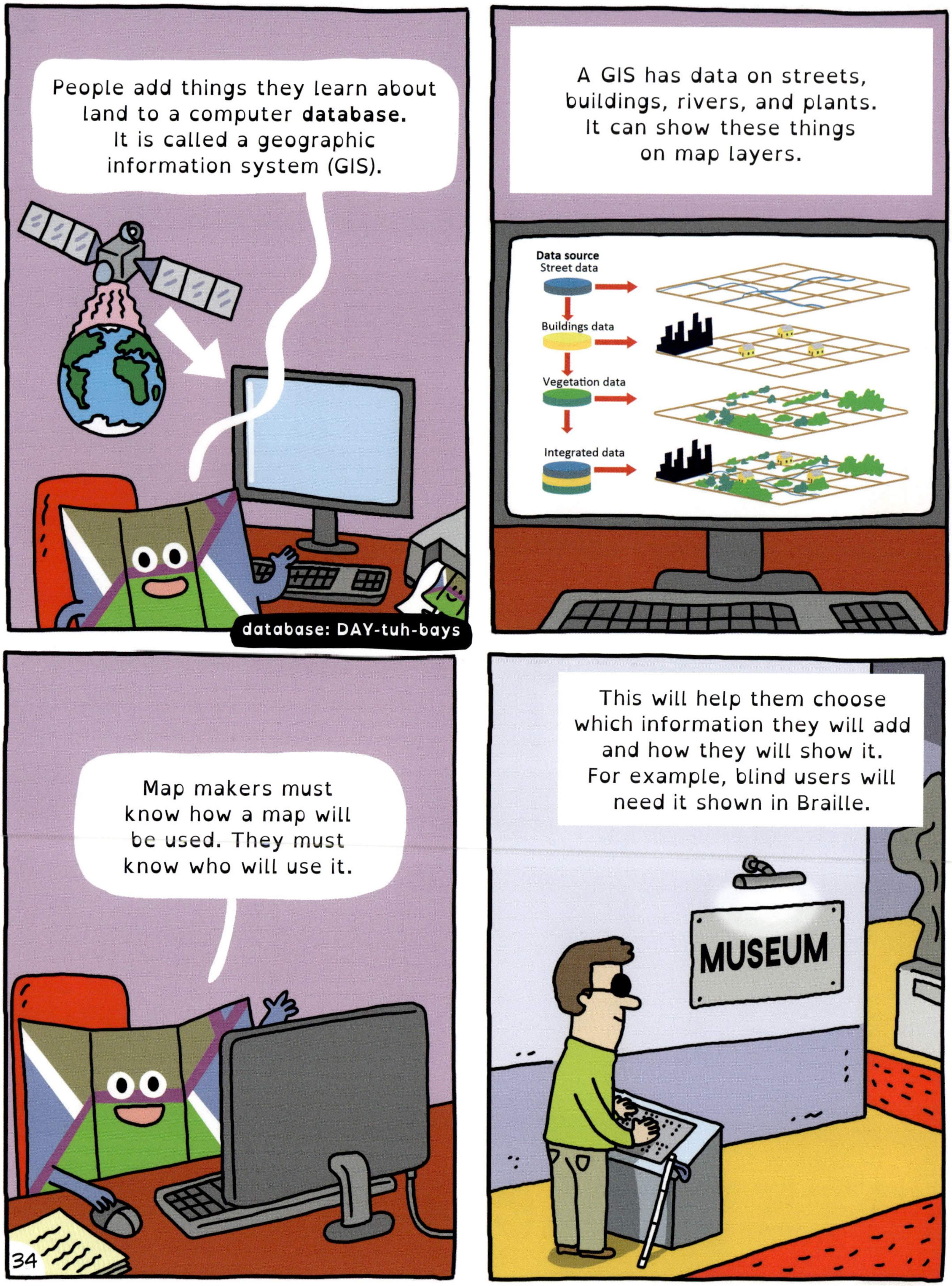
People add things they learn about land to a computer **database.** It is called a geographic information system (GIS).
database: DAY-tuh-bays
A GIS has data on streets, buildings, rivers, and plants. It can show these things on map layers.
Data source
Street data
Buildings data
Vegetation data
Integrated data
Map makers must know how a map will be used. They must know who will use it.
This will help them choose which information they will add and how they will show it. For example, blind users will need it shown in Braille.
MUSEUM

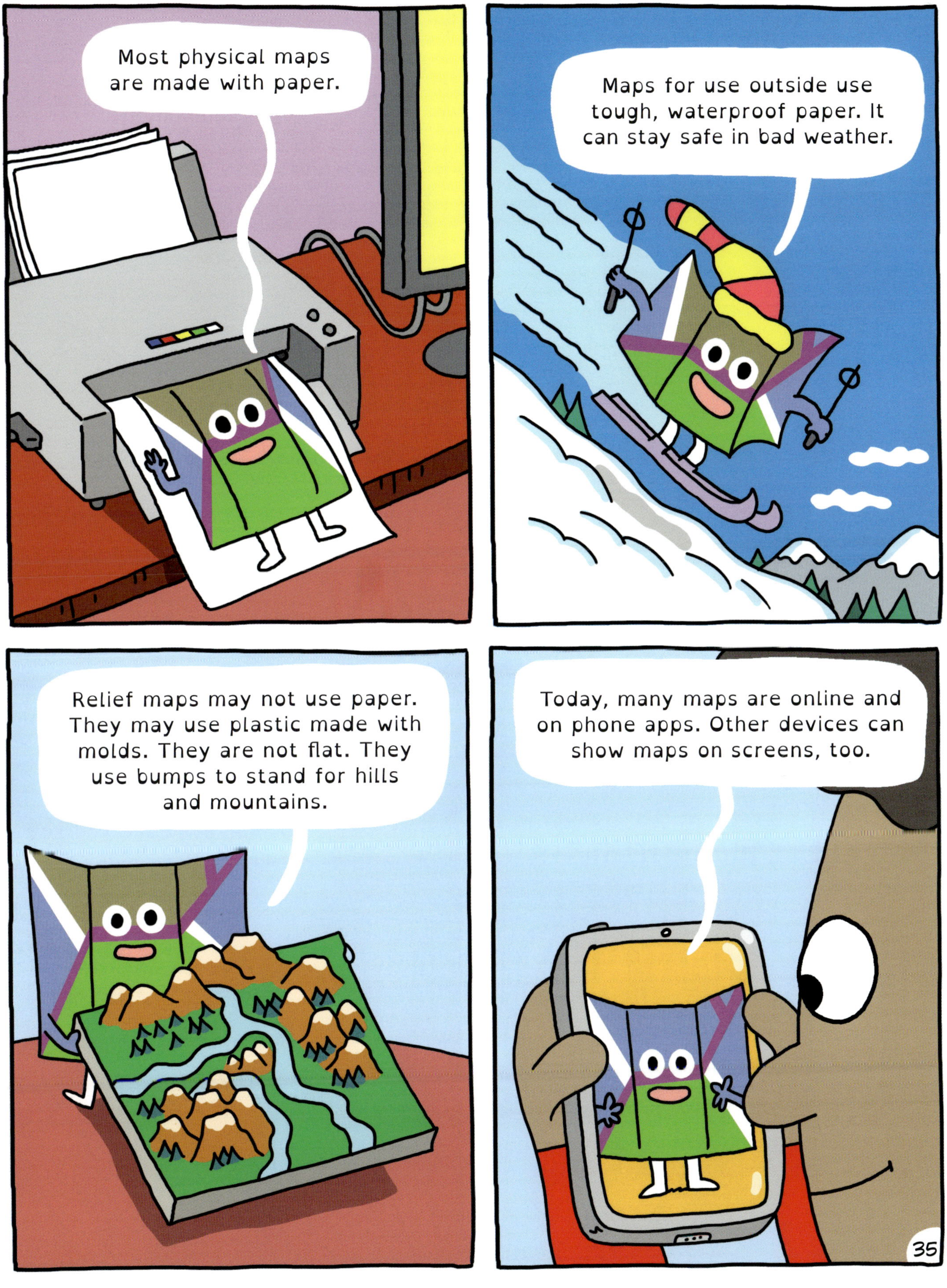
Most physical maps are made with paper.
Maps for use outside use tough, waterproof paper. It can stay safe in bad weather.
Relief maps may not use paper. They may use plastic made with molds. They are not flat. They use bumps to stand for hills and mountains.
Today, many maps are online and on phone apps. Other devices can show maps on screens, too.

MAPS TODAY

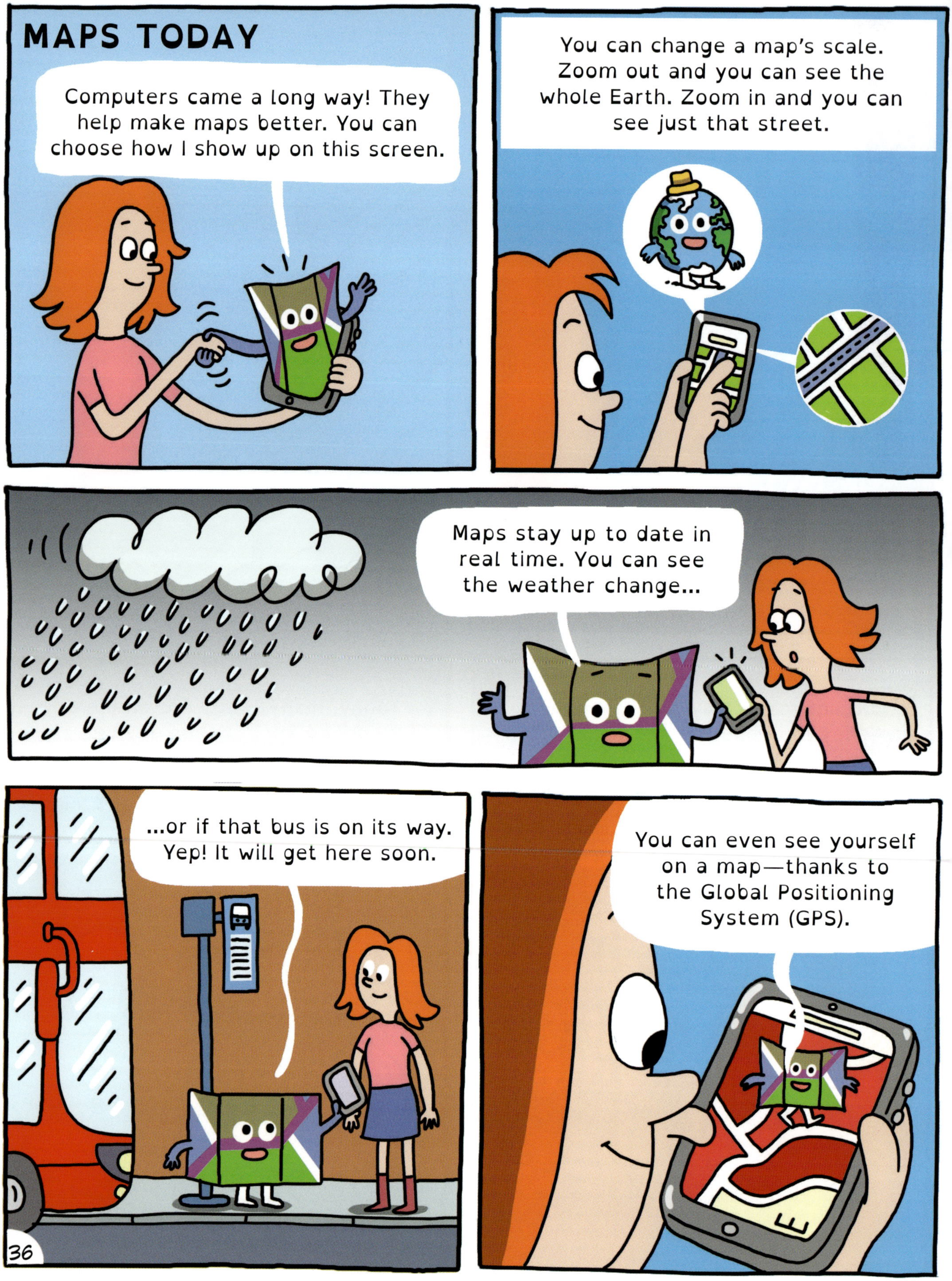
Computers came a long way! They help make maps better. You can choose how I show up on this screen.
You can change a map's scale. Zoom out and you can see the whole Earth. Zoom in and you can see just that street.
Maps stay up to date in real time. You can see the weather change...
...or if that bus is on its way. Yep! It will get here soon.
You can even see yourself on a map—thanks to the Global Positioning System (GPS).

GPS is a network. It is made up of satellites. It has been in space since the 1990s. It sends signals. It can find exact places on Earth.
If you have a GPS receiver—and most phones do—it is quite hard to get lost. But this phone's battery died!
IF YOU'RE here, YOU'RE PROBABLY LOST.
Apps can plot the best way for you to reach your destination. They track traffic. They tell you which way to go. They read maps for you!
Take the next road on the left.
Today, you can make maps, too! Map-making software helps you make maps from scratch or add things to maps made by someone else.
BEST ICE CREAM SHOP
SCARY DOG LIVES HERE
SHORT CUT TO SCHOOL
My surface changes all the time. New roads and cities are built. Rivers change widths and paths. Forests, deserts, and coasts change shape.
Maps need to stay up to date. The work of cartographers never stops!

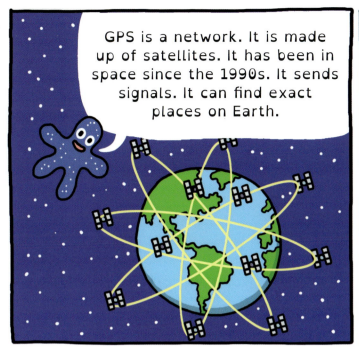

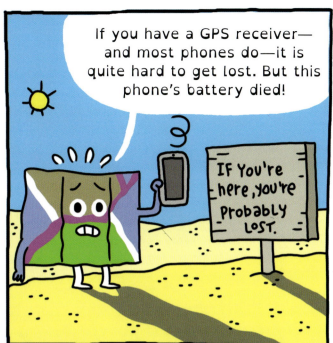

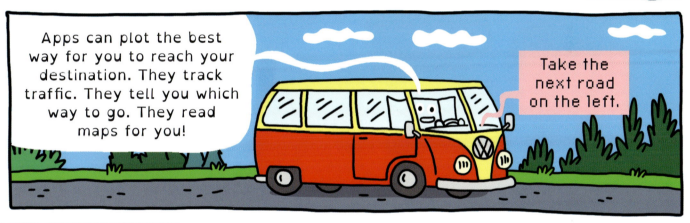

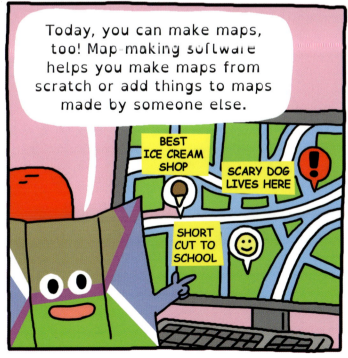

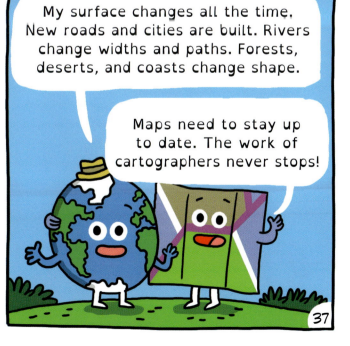

CAN YOU BELIEVE IT?!
In the Middle Ages, map makers wrote
"Here be dragons"
on maps. This meant the land had not been explored or it was not safe.

Jigsaw Puzzles

were first made around 1760 in London. They used maps glued on wood and cut in pieces. They were used to teach kids geography.

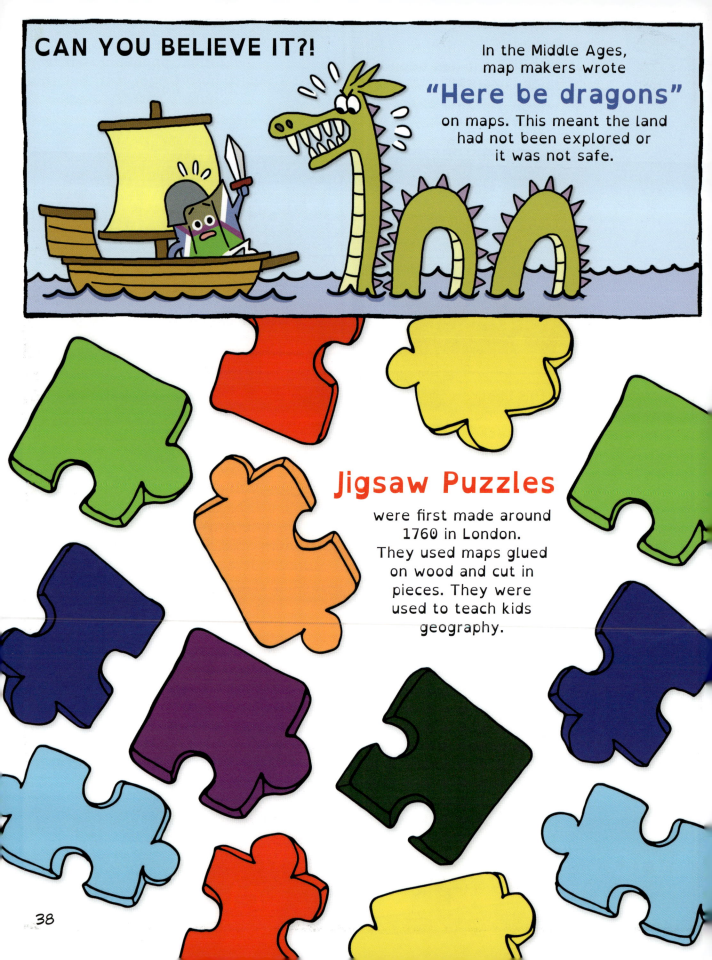

The Turin Papyrus Map may be **the oldest road map.** It was made in Egypt around 1160 BCE. It tells which roads cross rivers.

On European maps in the Middle Ages, **east was shown at the top of maps,** not north.

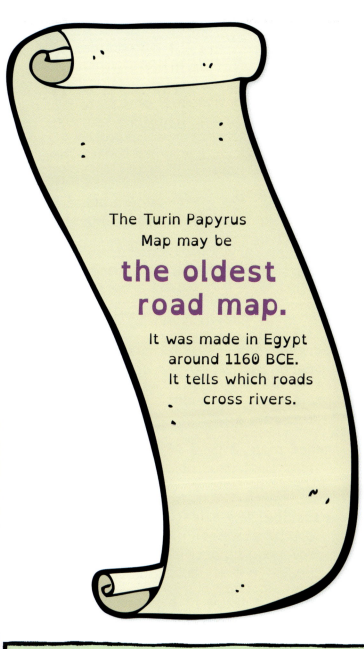

Past map makers might add **fake towns** on maps to catch people who copied their map without permission.

39

WORDS TO KNOW

app short for "application," is a computer program installed and run on a smartphone or other electronic devices.

cartographer a person who creates maps.

compass rose a map tool that tells the directions on a map using the letters N, E, S, and W.

compromise an acceptance of standards that are less than perfect.

contour lines lines on a map joining points of equal height.

coordinates letters and numbers used to indicate the position of something on a map.

database information held in a computer.

elevation height above sea level.

equator an imaginary line drawn on maps and globes halfway between the North and South Poles, dividing Earth into northern and southern hemispheres.

graticule a grid of lines representing meridians and parallels used on maps of the world.

grid a plane of intersecting lines that can be placed over a map to create a coordinate system.

inventory map a map that shows the locations of lots of the same kind of thing, such as gas stations or cinemas.

latitude the distance of a place north or south of the equator.

legend text on a map explaining the symbols used.

longitude the distance of a place east or west of the prime meridian.

meridian any line of longitude, circling Earth through the North and South Poles.

navigate find your way to a place.

parallel any line of latitude, circling Earth parallel to the equator.

projection representing Earth as a flat map.

relief map a type of topographic map that uses color to show the different heights of land.

satellite any celestial body that orbits a planet. In this book, we are referring to artificial (human-made) bodies in orbit around Earth.

symbol a shape or sign used to represent something.

thematic map a map that focuses on a particular topic, such as rainfall or population.

topographic map a map that shows the varying heights of different places.